First World War
and Army of Occupation
War Diary
France, Belgium and Germany

51 DIVISION
154 Infantry Brigade
Cameronians (Scottish Rifles)
6th Battalion
21 March 1915 - 31 May 1916

WO95/2887/6

The Naval & Military Press Ltd
www.nmarchive.com
Published in association with The National Archives

Published by

The Naval & Military Press Ltd

Unit 10 Ridgewood Industrial Park,

Uckfield, East Sussex,

TN22 5QE England

Tel: +44 (0) 1825 749494

www.naval-military-press.com

www.nmarchive.com

This diary has been reprinted in facsimile from the original. Any imperfections are inevitably reproduced and the quality may fall short of modern type and cartographic standards.

© Crown Copyright
Images reproduced by permission of The National Archives, London, England, 2015.

Contents

Document type	Place/Title	Date From	Date To
Heading	WO95/2887/6 6 Battalion Cameronians (Scottish Rifles)		
Heading	1/6 Scottish Rifles Vol XVIII To G H Q May 29th Replaced By 9th/71st		
Heading	8th Division 23rd Infy Bde 6th Bn Scottish Rifles Mar-May 1915 51 Div 154 Bde		
Heading	War Diary 6th Battn. The Cameronians (Scottish Rifles) March (21/31.3.15) 1915		
War Diary		21/03/1915	31/03/1915
Miscellaneous	Appendices I & II		
Miscellaneous	1/6th Cameronians	21/03/1915	21/03/1915
Miscellaneous	C Form (Duplicate). Messages And Signals.		
Heading	23rd Inf. Bde. 8th Div War Diary 6th Battn. The Cameronians (Scottish Rifles) April 1915		
War Diary		01/04/1915	30/04/1915
Heading	23rd Inf. 8th Div. Battn. Transferred To 154th Inf. Bde. 51st Div. 2.6.15 War Diary 6th Battn. The Cameronians (Scottish Rifles) May 1915		
War Diary		01/05/1915	31/05/1915
Heading	51st Division 154th Infy Bde 1-6th Bn Scottish Rifles Jun 1915 To May 1916 Amalgamated With 5 Bn 33 Div 19 Bde		
Heading	War Diary Of 1/6th Scottish Rifles From 1st June 1915 To 31st June 1915 Vol I		
War Diary		01/06/1915	12/06/1915
War Diary	Le Cornet Malo	13/06/1915	13/06/1915
War Diary	Festubert	14/06/1915	01/07/1915
Heading	War Diary Of 1/6th Scottish Rifles From 1st July 1915 To 31st July 1915 Vol II		
War Diary		01/07/1915	31/07/1915
Heading	War Diary Of 1/6th Scottish Rifles From 1st August 1915 To 31st August 1915 Vol III		
War Diary		01/08/1915	31/08/1915
Heading	57 Div. War Diary Of 1/6th Scottish Rifles From 1st Sept 1915 To 30th Sept 1915 Vol IV		
War Diary		01/09/1915	18/09/1915
War Diary	Sabbait	19/09/1915	30/09/1915
Miscellaneous	Special Order Of The Day	30/09/1915	30/09/1915
Heading	51st Div War Diary Of 1/6th Scottish Rifles From 1st October To 31st October 1915 Vol V		
War Diary		01/10/1915	31/10/1915
Miscellaneous	Special Order Of The Day	02/10/1915	02/10/1915
Miscellaneous	Special Order Of The Day By Field Marshal Sir J.D.P. French G.C.B. O.M. G.C.V.O. K.C.M.G. Commander-In-Chief British Army In The Field	04/10/1915	04/10/1915
Heading	51st Div 1/6th Scottish Rifles Nov & Dec 1915 Vol VI		
War Diary		01/11/1915	31/12/1915
Heading	51st Division 154th Infy Bde 1-6th Bn Scottish Rifles (Cameronians) Jan-Feb 1916		
Heading	1/6th Scottish Rifles Jan 1916 Vol VII		
War Diary		01/01/1916	31/01/1916

Heading	War Diary Of 6th Battalion The Cameronians (Scottish Rifles) From 1st February 1916 To 29th February 1916 Vol VIII		
War Diary		01/02/1916	29/02/1916
Heading	33rd Division 100th Infy Bde 51 Division 154 Bde 6th Bn Scottish Rifles (Cameronians) Mar-May 1916		
War Diary		01/03/1916	30/04/1916
Heading	1/6 Scottish Rifles Vol XVII		
War Diary		01/05/1916	31/05/1916

WO95/2887/6
6 Battalion Cameronians
(Scottish Rifles)

G.H.Q.
33

1/6 Scottish Rifles

Vol XVIII

~~XXXIII~~ (100)

to G.H.Q. May 29"
replaced by 9"/71 ½

18.P
17 piece

SERVED WITH { 8TH DIVISION
23RD INFY BDE

6TH BN SCOTTISH RIFLES
MAR - MAY 1915

51 DIV
154 Bde

23rd Inf.Bde.
8th Div.

Battn. disembarked
Havre from England
21.3.15.

Battn. joined Bde.
23.3.15.

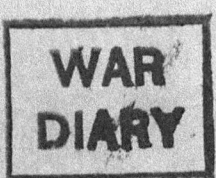

6th BATTN. THE CAMERONIANS (SCOTTISH RIFLES).

M A R C H

(21/31.3.15)

1 9 1 5

Attached:-

Appendices I & II.

WAR DIARY
or
INTELLIGENCE SUMMARY.

Army Form C. 2118.

6/Camerons

Hour, Date, Place	Summary of Events and Information	Remarks and references to Appendices
March 18th, 1915	Battalion disembarked at Havre about 8-30 a.m. Marched to No 2 Rest Camp. Inspected there on arrival by Commandant. Actual strength on disembarkation 30 Officers & 940 other ranks [which includes H/ 1 Medical Officer & 13 other ranks attached, 42 horses, 23 vehicles, 9 bicycles. Medical inspection of Bn. 3 men admitted to hospital] Buglers were armed with rifles as they had not been drawn for them at Home as Bn. Signallers. Lads down this hydro liner. Unarmed. Remained in Camp for night. Left March ? 4.?.	

Army Form C. 2118.

WAR DIARY
or
INTELLIGENCE SUMMARY.
(Erase heading not required.)

Instructions regarding War Diaries and Intelligence Summaries are contained in F.S. Regs., Part II. and the Staff Manual respectively. Title pages will be prepared in manuscript.

Hour, Date, Place	Summary of Events and Information	Remarks and references to Appendices
March 22nd, 1915.	At 1.30 am orders were received to entrain that day. [Man admitted to hospital.] Left camp at 3 pm & marched to station. Loaded transport wagons, horses & stores [on train.] Train left 6-30 pm. J.W.	See APPENDIX I
March 23rd, 1915.	Arrived LA GORGUE ESTAIRES about 5pm on 23rd March. Went into billets for the night. (Owing with rain.) Shortly after received march orders to following day. Learnt here that Bn was attached to 23rd Inf. Bde of 8th Division. This Bde includes 2nd Bn J. The Reg.t. J.W.	Ref M.F. BELGIUM HAZEBROUCK 1:100000 See APPENDIX II

Forms/C. 2118/10

WAR DIARY
or
INTELLIGENCE SUMMARY.
(Erase heading not required.)

Army Form C. 2118.

Hour, Date, Place	Summary of Events and Information	Remarks and references to Appendices
March 24th, 1915.	Battalion marched off at 10.30 a.m. & on arrival at H.Q. a Gen. HQ.th was directed to move to billets in FLEURBAIX. Arrived about 1 p.m. & occupied School at H.21. a.9.5. Very crowded there not being sufficient room for all units to lie down.	Ref BELGIUM - Sheet 36 1:40,000 Y.10 Y.10
March 25th, 1915	Battalion remained in billets — rifle inspections — cleaning up. In the afternoon received orders to take over fresh billets the following day. Arranged with O.C. 1/4th Middlesex Regt for 8 Officers & N.C.O's to visit trenches the following day & have writing from the O.C. Commander's. 2 Officers went through at paved at HAVRE arrived to-day	&c NCr

WAR DIARY
or
INTELLIGENCE SUMMARY.
(Erase heading not required.)

Army Form C. 2118.

Hour, Date, Place	Summary of Events and Information	Remarks and references to Appendices
March 25th/9.15	The following day took over extra billeting accommodation B - C - & Rampart. Moved to billets in RUE DELPIERRE. A Coy to billets in FLEURBAIX about H.21.d.3.2. D Coy & Headquarters in School at H.21.Q.9.5. Accomodation for B & C Coys mostly barns. Fresh straw was issued to these Coys. Billets made fairly comfortable. A Coy billeted in small house. Arranged with 1/4th Middlesex Regt to send 1 Waterer per Coy nightly to be attached to each Coy of 1/17 the Middlesex	BELGIUM. Sheet 36 1:40000

WAR DIARY
INTELLIGENCE SUMMARY

Hour, Date, Place	Summary of Events and Information	Remarks and references to Appendices
March 29, 1915	Regt. in the trenches. To continue in trenches. 7 men of B.2 7 men of 12 N.C.O's commenced gun instruction in trench mortar given admitted to Hospital B. alley, lyons(?) C.O. & adjutant visited section trenches held by 1/5th Middlesex Regt. This section can be entered by day with safety. Accompanied C.O. of 1/17th Middlesex to his mined known every portion of section. Very quiet — scarcely any firing. 4 platoons, 1 from A, B, C, D Coys went into the trenches this mgt for instruction, guides at CROIX MARÉCHAL	

WAR DIARY
or
INTELLIGENCE SUMMARY.
(Erase heading not required.)

Army Form C. 2118.

Hour, Date, Place	Summary of Events and Information	Remarks and references to Appendices

Cross roads who conducted them to the
Section of the trenches held by 1/7 to Middlesex
Regt.
The platoons remained in till about 7 p.m.
on following morning.
Arranged # to send 4 platoons in by
the following three nights, so that
when Bn takes over trenches from
1/7 th MIDDLESEX Regt, every man
will have shown the sights in the
trenches. Photographs, written party &
every officer of company from to be attached
men instructed to duty

Army Form C. 2118.

WAR DIARY
or
INTELLIGENCE SUMMARY.
(Erase heading not required.)

Instructions regarding War Diaries and Intelligence Summaries are contained in F.S. Regs., Part II. and the Staff Manual respectively. Title pages will be prepared in manuscript.

Hour, Date, Place	Summary of Events and Information	Remarks and references to Appendices
March 28th 1915	Sunday. Rifle Inspection. Voluntary Church Parade at 11 am. At about 12 noon Germans dropped 50 + 6 shells into FLEURBAIX. The billets occupied by A & B Coy were immediately evacuated. The men taking cover in adjoining fields. No casualties, but 1 man killed & 1 wounded were wanted unofficially to have occurred in 2nd Bn MIDDX E&S Ex Regt. Working party D 2 Officers 100 men furnished to night 28/29.	
March 29th 1915.	Rifle Inspection — cleaning kit &c. Adjutant visited 1st Bn Their Headquarters being about 1½ miles away. Working party 6 2 Officers 100 Men	

WAR DIARY
or
INTELLIGENCE SUMMARY.
(Erase heading not required.)

Army Form C. 2118.

Instructions regarding War Diaries and Intelligence Summaries are contained in F.S. Regs., Part II. and the Staff Manual respectively. Title pages will be prepared in manuscript.

Hour, Date, Place	Summary of Events and Information	Remarks and references to Appendices
March 28th 1915.	Furnished fatigues in work in No 3 Section. 2 men admitted to hospital to-day. Sgt. & men detached for duty with the Bath Horse now established at FLEURBAIX. 1 engineer & 3 others. Brig Genl. PENNY commanding 23rd Inf. Bde. visited the Coys stop to-day. The enemy to/ner a short lecture to the Officers & Sergeants of the Battalion. Fernando fired a few	

Forms/C. 2118/10

Army Form C. 2118.

WAR DIARY
or
INTELLIGENCE SUMMARY.
(Erase heading not required.)

Hour, Date, Place	Summary of Events and Information	Remarks and references to Appendices
	into FLEURBAIX. Bn had no casualties. Working party of 100 men & 2 officers detailed for work in No's station. To night two each Coy in the trenches 1 Platoon from each Coy in the trenches to night attached to 1/7th Middlesex Regt.	

WAR DIARY or INTELLIGENCE SUMMARY

Army Form C. 2118.

Hour, Date, Place	Summary of Events and Information	Remarks and references to Appendices
March 5th, 1915	3 men admitted Hospital to-day. 10.30 am the Coy Commanders were assembled to discuss the holding & procedure regarding the taking over of No 1. Section of the trenches at LA BOUTILLERIE at night. These trenches were originally dug by & that the Chaumeraux (District Alpha). The Bn. assembled at CROIX MARECHAL Cross roads, where the Coys were met by guides of the 1st Middlesex Coys of the 1/7 the MIDDLESEX Regt conducted it to their locates.	

WAR DIARY or INTELLIGENCE SUMMARY

Army Form C. 2118.

Hour, Date, Place	Summary of Events and Information	Remarks and references to Appendices
	A & B Coys 7th Frey. 1st line of Trenches C Coy in Support with two Platoons holding two redoubts & D Coy in reserve. The relief was exceedingly complicated. There were two battns. When Coy D 1/7th MIDDLESEX REGT had left Trenches carrying parties of D Coy 10th Bn. then battery R.E. stores to the Trenches. A very quiet night. Nothing relieved by shot burst of fire from our rifle & M.G. into the object of setting enemy.	

War Diary (continued)

Men & providing his working
Parties repairing damage

31 Mixed units

A P P E N D I C E S   I & II.

APPENDIX I

Officer Commanding

1/6th Cameronians

1. Please note that the Battalion (less 2 Platoons) under your command will entrain as detailed in Para 4 below.

2. Units must be very careful that every man in their unit is told the station and "point of Entrainment" before marching off from camp. Most of the numerous cases of men left behind have occurred through neglect of this precaution.

3. The entrance to Points Nos. 1, 2, and 4 is at No. 70 Cours de la Republique, and to Point 3 at the Boulevard d'Harfleur.

4. Place of entrainment **Gare des Marchandises.**

~~Gare Maritime.~~   Point No. 3

Time 16-30   Date 22nd March 1915.

Ration Party (strength 1 ~~officer~~ Officer 30 men) to report to Officer i/c Detail Issue Store at **Gare des Marchandises.**

~~Gare Maritime.~~   Point 6.

Time 16-00   Date 22nd March 1915.

N. B. — The time given is the hour at which units are to arrive **AT THE POINT** specified (i. e. place of entrainment).

5. As soon as orders for entrainment are received the units will at once notify the strength of the unit to the Officer i/c Detail Issue Store at place of entrainment.

6. Your attention is directed to the ~~attached~~ "Special Orders for units Passing through Havre Base", especially para. 7, and to "Standing orders for Entrainment" para 4.

Any further information about Entrainment can be obtained from the D A D R T

GARE DES VOYAGEURS

HAVRE.

Issued at 23-00
Date 21-3-15.

Para 7. 2 platoons will be left in camp and will entrain under separate orders, time & point will be notified later.

J. P. Barbertouch Major
D. A. Q. M. G.
HAVRE BASE.

"C" Form (Duplicate).
MESSAGES AND SIGNALS.

No. of Message 121

APPENDIX II

Service Instructions.

Handed in at Cya   Office   m. Received

TO 6th Bn Scots Rifs Tho
8 Division

Sender's Number	Day of Month	In reply to Number		AAA
SC175	23			

You will move your btn tomorrow 24 inst into billets in SAILLY BAC ST MAUR area aaa guide will meet your billeting party at 8 Divn hq in LA GORGUE at 9.0 am aaa Head of battn to pass the starting point 8 Divn hq at 10.30 am where a guide will meet you + conduct battalion to its billets aaa please acknowledge aaa addrsd 6th bn Scot rifles reptd 8 Divn

FROM
PLACE & TIME   23rd Inf Bde 5 47 pm

W.2594-283. 36,000 Pads-8/14. S. B. Ltd.-Forms/C.2123.

23rd Inf.Bde.
8th Div.

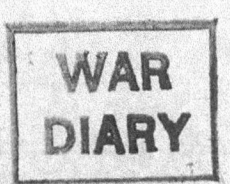

6th BATTN. THE CAMERONIANS (SCOTTISH RIFLES).

A P R I L

1 9 1 5

6/ Cameroons

Army Form C. 2118.

WAR DIARY
or
INTELLIGENCE SUMMARY.
(Erase heading not required.)

Instructions regarding War Diaries and Intelligence Summaries are contained in F.S. Regs., Part II. and the Staff Manual respectively. Title pages will be prepared in manuscript.

Hour, Date, Place	Summary of Events and Information	Remarks and references to Appendices
	line preventing his working parties repairing damage.	
April 1, 1915.	The Bath stood farms from 6am–9am. Nothing of evident occurred until about 1pm. The enemy started to shell Bath Headquarters [somewhat heavily]. It became necessary to remove the building & Headquarters. [This was done] to redoubt about 2 or 3 or 400 yds away. German guns fired 21 shells mostly [at this] shelling the road	

WAR DIARY
or
INTELLIGENCE SUMMARY.
(Erase heading not required.)

Army Form C. 2118.

Hour, Date, Place	Summary of Events and Information	Remarks and references to Appendices

Not general Shells struck the building & totally wrecking two rooms & damaging the room used as a firing room by the H.Q. Officers.

The C.O. sent & got painters trench in morning. Considerable amount of work required to be kept. Came the night man too tight before fire over.

One Casualty — man being shot in the mouth & instantly killed, he was shot in the trenches a bullet entering a loop hole.

WAR DIARY
or
INTELLIGENCE SUMMARY.

(Erase heading not required.)

Army Form C. 2118.

Hour, Date, Place	Summary of Events and Information	Remarks and references to Appendices
	Short bursts of fire were opened through out the night by 5th enemy working parties heard in this wire.	
	Stokes trench M.T. put in position if required.	
	Enemy throwing up flares at intervals through out night.	
	Trenches visited at night by Adjutant in Company with R.E. Officer who advised upon work to be done Sappers repair a lot of work the trenches	

Instructions regarding War Diaries and Intelligence Summaries are contained in F.S. Regs., Part II. and the Staff Manual respectively. Title pages will be prepared in manuscript.

WAR DIARY
or
INTELLIGENCE SUMMARY.

Army Form C. 2118.

Hour, Date, Place	Summary of Events and Information	Remarks and references to Appendices
April 2nd	Anthony killed but is some places & it a fresh parados is required for its full length. Other Repairs. Sandbags. Revetting. Drainage. Duty given Standard sofify it: Part II G/100). The night of the 1st/2nd was quiet except for occasional rifle fire as depicted in previous day. Battalion is under fire from about 5am At about 7-30 am Lt Genl PENNY Commanding 23rd INF BDE arrived at Batt Headquarters & visited the Trenches. Accompanied by CO & Adjutant	

WAR DIARY
or
INTELLIGENCE SUMMARY.

(Erase heading not required.)

Army Form C. 2118.

Hour, Date, Place	Summary of Events and Information	Remarks and references to Appendices

Reinforced himself as situated with what he saw hurriedly as regards the scenery of the new site. Has settled down to this life in trenches very quickly. The morning afterwards passed very quietly except for enemy snipers who were very persistent. Weather much colder with indications of snow.

A considerable amount of work is required by night from the Coys in [dugouts] & [trench] [lines]. These duties are to carry up rations — fuel

Water, R.E. stores &c. taken to the trenches.
The officers inform the various
that there are taken to the trenches,
there has been no firing between
our party & the enemy & the work
has thus been comparatively
expeditiously performed as the
carrying parties have usually
finished about 12 midnight.
1 other admitted to hospital to-day.

JWD

WAR DIARY
or
INTELLIGENCE SUMMARY
(Erase heading not required.)

Army Form C. 2118.

Hour, Date, Place	Summary of Events and Information	Remarks and references to Appendices
April 3rd 1915	The night of the 2/3rd April passed quietly. There were received shots after from the men directed on enemy's wire. The day passed without incident. Five men of B Coy shot [?] in the foot were relieved. In the evening A + B Coys [?] in the trenches by C + D Coys. Weather which has been dry however changed to rain + the trenches became very muddy. 1 man volunteered [?] to proceed up to the [?] [signed]	

WAR DIARY
or
INTELLIGENCE SUMMARY.

Army Form C. 2118.

(Erase heading not required.)

Hour, Date, Place	Summary of Events and Information	Remarks and references to Appendices
April 4 to 7/9/15	The night of the 3rd/4th to 4th/5th passed very quietly, there being practically no firing. Our men were engaged most of the night in pumping water out off the trenches & consequently were done up much more in the daylight. 4th done so heaped. Practically no firing all day, equally accounted for by the fact that to-day is Easter Sunday. Brigend PENNY visited us to-day. Official notification received to-day from 2nd Lt. A Mathau from Aunty Pen 1st April died from wounds	

WAR DIARY
or
INTELLIGENCE SUMMARY.
(Erase heading not required.)

Army Form C. 2118.

Hour, Date, Place	Summary of Events and Information	Remarks and references to Appendices
April 5th 1915	Worked yesterday & little privacy & very quiet all day. Nothing of enemy and nothing observed. 1 man admitted to hospital to-day. ff(a)	
	One man wounded about 8am this morning. He was working at the parapet & a stray bullet got him on left hand taking off thumb this finger. Rather wet & muddy day. In [event?] the day but about 7-8pm the enemy fired a few shells into FLEURBAIX. Our guns replied getting some [shells?]	

WAR DIARY
or
INTELLIGENCE SUMMARY.
(Erase heading not required.)

Hour, Date, Place	Summary of Events and Information	Remarks and references to Appendices
	Enemy is our front very peaceable at present except for a little sniping, there is little to say. About 5 pm today it commenced to rain very heavily & = a great deal of pumping was required to the trenches. Continued to rain most of tonight to trenches very muddy	
April 20 Aug 15th	Several Officers of 2/ NORTHAMPTONSHIRE REGT. the visited trenches either view to take them over that night	

WAR DIARY or INTELLIGENCE SUMMARY

Army Form C. 2118.

Hour, Date, Place	Summary of Events and Information	Remarks and references to Appendices

Rather a day. Major MOWATT slightly
the Bn. visited the redoubts & dugouts
but actually in the trench
One man wounded in the head rather
severely
Germans shelled FLEURBAIX somewhat
heavily pulling down several houses.
This happened about mid day.
Very cold wind all day but little
rain
Relieving trenches by 2/NORTH'N R Commenced

WAR DIARY
INTELLIGENCE SUMMARY
(Erase heading not required.)

Army Form C. 2118.

Hour, Date, Place	Summary of Events and Information	Remarks and references to Appendices

About 7-45 p.m. Raiding over menu Tay.
Smoothly but tho' night very dark.
Much helped by german flares.
About 9-50pm was able to telephone
H.Q. 23rd INF BDE that relief
was complete.
Marched back by Coys to BTN. ST
NM'K where the BDE is in divisional
Reserve a distance of about 4 miles,
The two Coys relieved from the trenches
arr'd very tired but no stragglers

WAR DIARY
or
INTELLIGENCE SUMMARY

(Erase heading not required.)

Army Form C. 2118.

Hour, Date, Place	Summary of Events and Information	Remarks and references to Appendices
April 7th, 1915.	Very quiet day. Coys left to themselves to clean up, kettle down after Trenches. Billets were cleaned up, fresh Latrines dug.	
April 8th, 1915.	Regiment for short route march of about 4 miles with 10 minutes interval between Coys. Weather rather showery between. 2 men admitted to hospital to-day	

WAR DIARY
or
INTELLIGENCE SUMMARY.
(Erase heading not required.)

Army Form C. 2118.

Hour, Date, Place	Summary of Events and Information	Remarks and references to Appendices
April 9th 1915.	4 men admitted to hospital to-day. Coys exercised in close order drill, handling of arms, saluting & physical exercises. Weather rather wet & showery. B & Coy men paid to-day.	
April 10th 1915.	6 men admitted to hospital to-day. Coys route marching to-day. Weather warm & sunny. Received orders to move into Night B^{n} area on relieving 85th Bde. viz. 2/Devons - 2/Sco Rifles - 1/Middx	4/4/15

Army Form C. 2118.

WAR DIARY
or
INTELLIGENCE SUMMARY.
(Erase heading not required.)

Instructions regarding War Diaries and Intelligence Summaries are contained in F.S. Regs., Part II. and the Staff Manual respectively. Title pages will be prepared in manuscript.

Hour, Date, Place	Summary of Events and Information	Remarks and references to Appendices
	go into trenches, the remaining three Bns 2/W YORK R - 6/Sco RIFLES & 2/MIDDL'X being in B0E reserve. Bns are grouped for trench relief as follows 2/DEVON·R } 2/W.YORK R } No 3 Section 2/Sco RIFLES } 6/Sco RIFLES } No 2 Section 2/MIDDL'X.R } 1/MIDDL'X.R. } No 1 Section	

WAR DIARY
or
INTELLIGENCE SUMMARY.
(Erase heading not required.)

Army Form C. 2118.

Hour, Date, Place	Summary of Events and Information	Remarks and references to Appendices
	1. Coy B duty in the trenches for 6 days. Arrangements for taking over trenches by shade by Mutual agreement between O.S.C. Battalions arrived. *(sgd)*	
April 11, 1915.	Has been admitted to hospital to-day. Divine service held in billets at 12 noon. Bright sunny day. 525 detailed as working parties under R.E. to-night. *(sgd)*	

WAR DIARY
or
INTELLIGENCE SUMMARY

(Erase heading not required.)

Army Form C. 2118.

Hour, Date, Place	Summary of Events and Information	Remarks and references to Appendices
April 10th, 1915.	During the night of 11th/12th the working parties were sniped afterwards & fire there was killed & one wounded in section 6 of the trenches. In addition to above Casualties 4 men were admitted to hospital this morning. In the evening the BDE took over right BDE area from 25th BDE. The 2/SCO RIF relieved the No.2 Section of the Trenches the 6th SCO RIF moved into billets at RUE DU BOIS in N.2.13 & H 33. C. Batt moved off from BAC ST MAUR at 7-15 pm arriving at new billets at 8-30 pm	

Army Form C. 2118.

WAR DIARY
or
INTELLIGENCE SUMMARY.
(Erase heading not required.)

Instructions regarding War Diaries and Intelligence Summaries are contained in F.S. Regs., Part II. and the Staff Manual respectively. Title pages will be prepared in manuscript.

Hour, Date, Place	Summary of Events and Information	Remarks and references to Appendices
	Transport was loaded Lunches at mess as it had to be moving by 1-15pm. It was the road for our opening out of the Needles for a Fleets, men being in Boys Camp with plenty of straw.	
April 15th 1915	3 Men admitted Hospital to-day. Warm day. boys did physical drill in forms where they were well shielded. Fatigue parties busy all day endeavouring to clean drains yet stagnant water run away.	

Army Form C. 2118.

WAR DIARY
or
INTELLIGENCE SUMMARY.
(Erase heading not required.)

Instructions regarding War Diaries and Intelligence Summaries are contained in F.S. Regs., Part II. and the Staff Manual respectively. Title pages will be prepared in manuscript.

Hour, Date, Place	Summary of Events and Information	Remarks and references to Appendices
April 14th, 1915.	5.3 Men admitted Hospital to day. Very quiet day. No shelling. Very busy with drains endeavouring to get part water away north. Some success. Coy Commanders visited trenches held by 2nd S.R to-day as a preparation for taking them over on 18th. HWV	
April 15th, 1915	2 men admitted Hospital to day. Draining operations continued. Coys did physical drill etc. GCD	

Army Form C. 2118.

WAR DIARY
or
INTELLIGENCE SUMMARY.
(Erase heading not required.)

Instructions regarding War Diaries and Intelligence Summaries are contained in F.S. Regs., Part II. and the Staff Manual respectively. Title pages will be prepared in manuscript.

Hour, Date, Place	Summary of Events and Information	Remarks and references to Appendices
April 18th, 1915	1 man admitted to hospital to day 4 men went away to day to be attached to 173rd Coy R.E. The best of these men will be transferred to R.E. as Miners to be employed on sapping operations. yyws	
April 19th, 1915	Coys went for a short route march of about 3 miles. Remainder of day hyrotraining water. C.O & Adjutant arranged details of relief of 2w Bn to take place on Sunday night	

WAR DIARY
or
INTELLIGENCE SUMMARY.
(Erase heading not required.)

Army Form C. 2118.

Hour, Date, Place	Summary of Events and Information	Remarks and references to Appendices
	Enemy dropped about 30 shells between 19"D" of SCO RIF & RUE DE BOIS. They were probably endeavouring to find position of 35th Sty. R.F.A. in RUE DE BOIS which had been firing. No casualties. First 2 German shells did not burst.	
April 18th, 1915.	2 men admitted hospital yesterday. 23 men who had been trained as bomb throwers returned to Bn yesterday. S.O. then headquarters at corresponding no. of men sent to be trained.	

WAR DIARY
or
INTELLIGENCE SUMMARY.
(Erase heading not required.)

Army Form C. 2118.

Hour, Date, Place	Summary of Events and Information	Remarks and references to Appendices
April 18th, 1915.	To-night both over No 3 sector & the trenches from 2nd SCO RIF. The relief was very pretty repeatedly perfumed. The first Coy arrived & Pud Coy 2/Lt S.R Spry 10pm to be conducted to the trenches & by 9-25pm the relief was completed. Quiet night. Little firing. #H	By OD
April 19th 1915.	Shortly after day break this morning Lce Cngn was killed being shot through the head which he had incautiously raised over the parapet. Later on, one man was shot through	

WAR DIARY
or
INTELLIGENCE SUMMARY.
(Erase heading not required.)

Army Form C. 2118.

Hour, Date, Place	Summary of Events and Information	Remarks and references to Appendices
	Aptrea. By doing the same thing considerable amounts of work was done in the trenches improving, thickening the parapet, building parados & extra dug outs. Work however much delayed owing to the shortage of R.E. Stores. Enemy's snipers active all day. At night as returns were driving enemy opened fire with 2 machine guns but the casualties. After about 30 minutes desultory firing it ceased.	

Instructions regarding War Diaries and Intelligence Summaries are contained in F. S. Regs., Part II. and the Staff Manual respectively. Title pages will be prepared in manuscript.

Army Form C. 2118.

WAR DIARY
or
INTELLIGENCE SUMMARY.
(Erase heading not required.)

Instructions regarding War Diaries and Intelligence Summaries are contained in F.S. Regs., Part II. and the Staff Manual respectively. Title pages will be prepared in manuscript.

Hour, Date, Place	Summary of Events and Information	Remarks and references to Appendices
April 20th, 1915	The C.O. & Capan. Grieves arrived about 4-30 p.m. & the burial of Pte Johnson & the other man who was killed in the morning took place. An uneventful day. Germans in front of our Section very quiet. A little of shelling on No 1 Section. Great shortage of R.E. stores & consequently very little work done in the trenches. The enemy usually open fire with a M.G. about 9 pm on road where our rations arrive by, but to-night no firing at all.	

Army Form C. 2118.

WAR DIARY
or
INTELLIGENCE SUMMARY.
(Erase heading not required.)

Instructions regarding War Diaries and Intelligence Summaries are contained in F. S. Regs., Part II. and the Staff Manual respectively. Title pages will be prepared in manuscript.

Hour, Date, Place	Summary of Events and Information	Remarks and references to Appendices
April 21st 1915	The night of the 20/21st was the most quiet night yet spent in trenches by this Bn. Practically no firing by enemy who also sent up no flares owing to their usual Creature. Brig Genl PINNEY visited trenches to-day. Our Artillery shelled German trenches to-day & damaged their parapet. 2 O.R. damaged their parapet. 2 Men admitted to hospital to-day.	

WAR DIARY or INTELLIGENCE SUMMARY.

Army Form C. 2118.

Hour, Date, Place	Summary of Events and Information	Remarks and references to Appendices
April 29th 1915	There was a good deal of firing by enemy during the night. 2 St John's Coy. S.O.1 working parties in rear. No.2 Section had 3 or 4 casualties. Shortly after daybreak one man killed in the trench. Party of 9 men per man who was employed in clearing out a ditch close to 35" H.Q. of war wounded by a stray bullet. Conference at 10 a.m. in Bn. H.Q.rs by Brigadier PINNEY. Our guns registering on enemy trenches in front of No.2 Section. Very heavy musketry fire, enemy's parapet being enlarged. J.L.	

WAR DIARY
or
INTELLIGENCE SUMMARY.

(Erase heading not required.)

Hour, Date, Place	Summary of Events and Information	Remarks and references to Appendices
April 22nd 1915	No casualties during night 21st/22nd which passed very quietly. In the afternoon enemy guns commenced shelling evidently trying to find a battery established near dugout, & it became necessary for 2 Platoons A Coy to leave their billets & take to dug outs. The Billet was hit by splinters of Shell. Several shells fell in the meadow in which the dug outs were situated but no casualties.	

WAR DIARY
INTELLIGENCE SUMMARY.
(Erase heading not required.)

Army Form C. 2118.

Hour, Date, Place	Summary of Events and Information	Remarks and references to Appendices

At 1 during the evening 3 platoons B Coy in the trenches were relieved by 3 platoons B Coy of 6" — 3 platoon Suffolk Brigade + 1 platoon Roy. Irish Rifles. This party under special orders is substituting Chevaux de Frise instead. By the H.C. wire entanglements from 16J sector R.P.

Y.W.D.

WAR DIARY
or
INTELLIGENCE SUMMARY.
(Erase heading not required.)

Army Form C. 2118.

Hour, Date, Place	Summary of Events and Information	Remarks and references to Appendices
26th April 1915	Enemy shelled Hospital to day. A good deal of firing during night of 23/24 April 4 sgt 4 men Gloucester Rants Fusiliers 10th Infsdn were put over than being killed. Very quiet day. Germans made no attempt to fire on Battery established near Bn. H.Q. In the evening the 2/ NORTHANTS REGT relieved us in trenches	

WAR DIARY
or
INTELLIGENCE SUMMARY.

(Erase heading not required.)

Army Form C. 2118.

Hour, Date, Place	Summary of Events and Information	Remarks and references to Appendices
	The relief was very much delayed. The relieving Bn arrived Rafts in at 8-15pm. By 10pm the relief was accomplished. Five men have been killed & four been wounded in C Coy after leaving their trenches on way back to RUE PETILLON. Bn arrived in new billets at STAPLE about 11-30pm. Ek. Div. in Divisional Reserve. Signed	

WAR DIARY
or
INTELLIGENCE SUMMARY.

(Erase heading not required.)

Hour, Date, Place	Summary of Events and Information	Remarks and references to Appendices
April 24th 1915	No parade to-day except rifle shot instructors. Voluntary C of E Service at 9 am. Been decided to-day for us to move to new billets in vicinity of DOULIEU to-morrow.	
April 25th 1915	Opperations as laid down. Raining. On parade to-day. Marched at 4 pm to new billets near DOULIEU. Arrived about 5.15 pm.	

Army Form C. 2118.

WAR DIARY
or
INTELLIGENCE SUMMARY.
(Erase heading not required.)

Army Form C. 2118.

Hour, Date, Place	Summary of Events and Information	Remarks and references to Appendices
April 29th 1915.	Keysford Billets but authenticated Fgas Battalion received to-day in advancing over country as if under artillery fire. Each Coy had 2 Platoons in 1st line & 2 in second. Platoons were in line of sections on a frontage about 300 yds. There were numerous obstacles in the shape of hedges, ditches & small streams.	

WAR DIARY
or
~~INTELLIGENCE~~ SUMMARY.
(Erase heading not required.)

Army Form C. 2118.

Hour, Date, Place	Summary of Events and Information	Remarks and references to Appendices
April 29th, 1915	The advance was rather too slow as section all crossed obstacles in one place instead of opening out getting through in as many places as possible. At conclusion of exercise officers & N.C.O's were assembled to hear Sir PINNEY who was superintending the exercise, give his criticisms on the above mentioned points. Heavy artillery fire heard all day from the YPRES direction	

Army Form C. 2118.

WAR DIARY
or
INTELLIGENCE SUMMARY.
(Erase heading not required.)

Hour, Date, Place	Summary of Events and Information	Remarks and references to Appendices
	All officers were assembled in the afternoon at Bn. H.Q. for a conference regarding training for the proposed offensive operations to be undertaken by the 1st Army.	
April 28th, 1915.	Very hot day. Batt went for route march of about 5 miles in the morning. In the afternoon musketry instruction was carried out.	

Army Form C. 2118.

WAR DIARY
or
INTELLIGENCE SUMMARY.
(Erase heading not required.)

Instructions regarding War Diaries and Intelligence Summaries are contained in F. S. Regs., Part II. and the Staff Manual respectively. Title pages will be prepared in manuscript.

Hour, Date, Place	Summary of Events and Information	Remarks and references to Appendices
April 29th 1915.	The men admitted to hospital to-day. "7pm" In the morning arms drill, Physical training, Musketry was carried out. In the afternoon a short route march followed by an advance across country under artillery fire was performed. The exercise was carried out over the same ground as on 27. The advance was a considerable improvement on the last. It was carried out in about half the time as the men were much quicker to surmount/obstacles. 9/10	

(9 29 6) W 4141—463 100,000 9/14 H W V Forms/C. 2118/10

Army Form C. 2118.

WAR DIARY
or
INTELLIGENCE SUMMARY.
(Erase heading not required.)

Instructions regarding War Diaries and Intelligence Summaries are contained in F. S. Regs., Part II. and the Staff Manual respectively. Title pages will be prepared in manuscript.

Hour, Date, Place	Summary of Events and Information	Remarks and references to Appendices
April 30th, 1915.	Very hot to-day. Battalion went a route march f about 5 miles in the morning. In the afternoon, Coys at the disposal of Coy commanders for musketry etc. One man admitted to hospital to day. Cw-mont × 5 w. 7 sick 1 + 40	

23rd Inf.Bde.
8th Div.

Battn. transferred
to 154th Inf.Bde.
51st Div. 2.6.15.

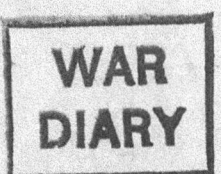

6th BATTN. THE CAMERONIANS (SCOTTISH RIFLES).

M A Y

1 9 1 5

Army Form C. 2118.

6/Commences

WAR DIARY
or
INTELLIGENCE SUMMARY.
(Erase heading not required.)

Instructions regarding War Diaries and Intelligence Summaries are contained in F. S. Regs., Part II. and the Staff Manual respectively. Title pages will be prepared in manuscript.

Hour, Date, Place	Summary of Events and Information	Remarks and references to Appendices
May 1st, 1915.	Early this morning about 4.30 am very heavy shell fire heard from direction of PORT ARTHUR, this which lasted about 1 hour. About 6.30 am a message was received stating that the Brigade was fit and if arms the ready to move at a moments notice the receipt of the orders were sent to O.C Coys to this effect. Blankets were collected by Transport & stacked in a shed in R or Q Pilots. Meanwhile men	

WAR DIARY
or
INTELLIGENCE SUMMARY.

(Erase heading not required.)

Army Form C. 2118.

Instructions regarding War Diaries and Intelligence Summaries are contained in F.S. Regs., Part II. and the Staff Manual respectively. Title pages will be prepared in manuscript.

Hour, Date, Place	Summary of Events and Information	Remarks and references to Appendices

With drawn from men, ordered, packed up wagons, &c. So On that were in a state of readiness within an hour of receiving order.

Shortly after, second order received that move to return to billets. About 8:30 am information received from 23rd INF Bde that enemy shelled our men PORT ARTHUR to PONT LOGY also on RUE DU BOIS, Neufchatel at a moments notice ready to turn out at a moments notice.

WAR DIARY
or
INTELLIGENCE SUMMARY.
(Erase heading not required.)

Army Form C. 2118.

Instructions regarding War Diaries and Intelligence Summaries are contained in F.S. Regs., Part II. and the Staff Manual respectively. Title pages will be prepared in manuscript.

Hour, Date, Place	Summary of Events and Information	Remarks and references to Appendices
	behind our lines. A/P interpretation of an attack. Enemy also reported to be filling up dense screen of smoke opposite A & B sub-sections but apparently to conceal movements. Shortly after 10 a.m. message received that normal conditions might be resumed. Remainder of day spent into Physical Training in ground. Message received that all ranks to proceed to Lecture from 5 to 7 p.m. has been instituted from to-day.	

WAR DIARY or INTELLIGENCE SUMMARY

Army Form C. 2118.

Hour, Date, Place	Summary of Events and Information	Remarks and references to Appendices
May 2nd 1915.	At 8-30 a.m. Orders received for Bn to move from Flêtre at ESTAIRES. [Billeting party went on in advance at Flêtre also.] Marched at 12-15 p.m. arriving ESTAIRES at 5:00 p.m. Found Billets very dirty & the next day spent in cleaning up. About 2:30 p.m. orders received that the Brigade was to take over C→D Lines to be held from 2nd/7th N.F. B.D. 1 = Sykes 2/ DEVON Regt. Y/ MIDD'Y Regt. & SCO. RIF = to take over trenches, the other Bns. Bde.	

WAR DIARY
INTELLIGENCE SUMMARY

Hour, Date, Place	Summary of Events and Information	Remarks and references to Appendices
May 4th, 1915	Received orders about 10 a.m. that the Bn. the ready to move in the afternoon & about 9 a.m. a further order that the Bn. was to move at 11 p.m. A billeting party to take [Bn] billets between STILLY & RUE d QUESNE. Billeting party went off at 11 a.m. under Major SMITH. About 11 a.m. orders received ordering the Bn. at 1 p.m. March table attached. Marched at 1 p.m. & arrived new billets at 3 p.m. Rather crowded. Following working parties supplied tonight. 1 Officer 450 men 3 Coy. 2 Officers 400 men B Coy. 2 Officers + 70	

WAR DIARY
or
INTELLIGENCE SUMMARY.
(Erase heading not required.)

Army Form C. 2118.

Hour, Date, Place	Summary of Events and Information	Remarks and references to Appendices
May 5th 1915	10 men C. by. About 4 hrs heavy thunderstorm. All Coys went for short run before breakfast. After breakfast, Coys exercised in Coy drill, Physical Training & musketry. Very hot retiring day. In the evening C.O. & Adjutant out attended conference at Bde Headquarters concerning proposed Offensive Operations following morning. Party supplied 1 Officer & 50 men D Coy. This too party regining bythly	

WAR DIARY
or
INTELLIGENCE SUMMARY.
(Erase heading not required.)

Army Form C. 2118.

Hour, Date, Place	Summary of Events and Information	Remarks and references to Appendices
May 6th, 1915	Slightly wet & rather colder. 6 men admitted to hospital to-day. Coy commanders assembled at 9 a.m. Various admin. items put in force into regarding preparation for offensive operations. Bandolier extra ammunition, drawn, extra wire cutters issued to men. Regarding men returning also regarding returns. Delays to be caused either of men. Was broken which had previously been issued were returned for not fitting bayt L.E. Rifle, with which the Batt is armed. In the evening Bay Division orders received regarding assembly of Bay & joint arct orders to attend Bde	

WAR DIARY
or
INTELLIGENCE SUMMARY.
(Erase heading not required.)

Army Form C. 2118.

Hour, Date, Place	Summary of Events and Information	Remarks and references to Appendices
May 4th, 1915	N.C.O.s at 10 a.m. to morrow for a Conference. Day spent in making arrangements [Blankets, packs, Camp kettles were collected. Blankets were stacked in Mr Pilat, packs, Camp kettles packed on Transport. Tent rack to Transport lines. In accordance with B.O.s orders, water carts were filled. Tent with two off the water duty personnel to reach in the Orchard at CROIX BLANC - [ ] of PUR DU BOIS. Bombs were drawn. Issued to the Bn bombers. Instruction was given in use of Rifle	

Army Form C. 2118.

WAR DIARY
or
INTELLIGENCE SUMMARY.
(Erase heading not required.)

Hour, Date, Place	Summary of Events and Information	Remarks and references to Appendices

May 8th — 10th.

Paraded to 2 N.C.O's per Coy.
About 5:30pm an order was received
saying that the operation was postponed
for 24 hours, that the orders already
issued held good for following day.

The morning of was spent in completing any
deficiencies in ammunition, rations, respirators
etc.
At 2pm a conference of all officers was
held & the orders issued for the operation
carefully gone into.
At 9:15pm the Battalion marched off [?]

From Billets for the position of assembly. Northern Humerons been reconnoitred by Senior Officer Major SHAY.

Order of march   A - C - B - D and Ba Bombers
Carrying party.

Carrying party of 6 attached contained Coy
O/R i Sergt, Coy Cook, Officers servants,
Grocers Mess useful men for carrying
rations, Water, ammunition etc.
Arrived an assembly trenches in rear of CELLAR
FM about 6.25 pm.
An Officer with a N.C.O from each Coy
had preceded the Bn to as each Coy
came up they were directed to the trenches

WAR DIARY
or
INTELLIGENCE SUMMARY.
(Erase heading not required.)

Hour, Date, Place	Summary of Events and Information	Remarks and references to Appendices

the occupation was quietly & perpetually done, the war log being in its trenches by 8-6 p.m. The hostile was heightened & thickened during the night, wire drawn from CELLM & raised.

The 2 W Bn SCO RIF were assembled in trenches on our right, the dividing line being the communication trench from RYE - PETILLON to the section 2 B. the fir trenches. The right & the 8 W 9 Tn passed quietly. It very cold in trenches & there got little sleep.

At 5am the bombardment of enemy
trenches commenced. Noise nothing like
as bad as one had been led to expect,
as General Gun is seemed to be that
the bombardment was not to intense as
at NEUVE CHAPELLE
Shortly after bombardment commenced, made
arrangements with 2nd Bn for communication
as to own men to follow our advance when
advance commenced.
About 7am. Brigdr PINNEY Commanding
23rd Inf: Bde of fact explained that
RIFLE BRIGADE & 25th Inf Bde were
not getting in & required reinforcements

He had ordered the 9th Bn. SCO RIF to
support them as they were the nearest
available Batt. that the 8th SCO RIF were
therefore by[?]follow 2/ W. YORKS. REGT
instead

9th Bn moved off to the right to clear
CELLAR FM & then advanced to
the line of assembly trenches
About 4-15 a.m. the two leading Coys of the
Bn. A & C moved to the right into
trenches vacated by 2nd RB in readiness
to move.
Attacking 2nd TOTV from position. It
was it was difficult until to destroy until

WAR DIARY
or
INTELLIGENCE SUMMARY.

(Erase heading not required.)

Hour, Date, Place	Summary of Events and Information	Remarks and references to Appendices

Our Bn from another that was seen, was very
lines of men in single file entering
assembly trenches about 500 yds to our
right. 2nd Lt COLVILLE got into
communication with the 2nd wheel
turned to the 2/ DEVON R REGT
orderlies to a similar men then sent
men to these trenches Signal the
advance 2/3/ W YORKS R.
At about 7.0 am an order received from
295 INF BDE that Bn bombers
were despatched O.C. 2/ SCO RIF in
fire trenches
Lieut GREY now in command the
party consisted of 24 bombers

WAR DIARY
or
INTELLIGENCE SUMMARY.
(Erase heading not required.)

Army Form C. 2118.

Hour, Date, Place	Summary of Events and Information	Remarks and references to Appendices

Light carriers, 46 men in day out event.
At about 12.30pm orders received that extra
front carriers were required. These, dispatched
at once.
About this same hour, an order received
saying that we was drew air is present
position i.e. assembly trenches until further
orders.
At about 2pm. enemy's guns which had
been very busy all day commenced
searching for our trenches. It for about
half an hour shells were bursting in the
next field to that in which assembly trenches
were cut & the majority of shells dropped

WAR DIARY
or
INTELLIGENCE SUMMARY

Army Form C. 2118.

Summary of Events and Information.

5.0 P.M. gas from the flash of our rifles. Two or three men were hit by splinters.

No definite information at this time was forthcoming on either side of the action, but that our casualties were very heavy was obvious by the continuous stream of wounded turning to the rear along the communication trench.

No orders to move were received. It was now known that our advance had come to a standstill.

A heavy bombardment presently recommenced shortly after 9 p.m. continued till about 3:30 a.m. It was estimated that approximately 100 shells were fired during that time, the majority of them bursting either short 20 yds of our trenches, in front, behind, and on the flash, but there were only two direct hits on the trenches themselves.

WAR DIARY
or
INTELLIGENCE SUMMARY
(Erase heading not required).

Army Form C. 2118.

Hour, Date, Place.	Summary of Events and Information.	Remarks and References to Appendices.

The Dr escaped in the most lucky way from this rather trying ordeal. Only 2 or 3 men to were hit as the result of their bombardment. At about 3.30pm enemy guns shelled their line & divided their attention to their targets. Firing was practically all night until about day light when it practically ceased. At about 7pm the 3rd SCO RIF returned to their original assembly trenches on our right. At about 10pm 1st G.R.A of Mr. Roay Hofbrookein a state of absolute exhaustion. The bombing party had been so employed in capturing German trenches, & after very heavy fighting had to retire in face of superior numbers. That total casualties in the bombing party

Army Form C. 2118.

WAR DIARY
or
INTELLIGENCE SUMMARY
(Erase heading not required).

Hour, Date, Place.	Summary of Events and Information.	Remarks and References to Appendices.

Wheel confirmed broken, took carrier's bayonet event was 10 wounded & missing.

On early morning of 10th returns these were revised to three. No costing was done during these operations.

The morning of 6th inst. passed very quietly there being practically no firing. The principal signs. Stretcher bearers were worked men.

About 12-45 p.m. an order was received for the Brigade stores to pass junction at M.12.a.9.9 Humac then. Arrived about 9 p.m. At night A. & C. Coys took over F.2 section of trenches from 6th Cameron H'flanders, B & D Coys remaining in Humac in support

WAR DIARY
or
INTELLIGENCE SUMMARY
(Erase heading not required).

Army Form C. 2118.

Hour, Date, Place.	Summary of Events and Information.	Remarks and References to Appendices.

The total casualties in the above three operations was 1 man killed, 24 wounded & 1 missing. Despite these small losses the period described in this narrative was a rather trying one for the young & comparatively inexperienced troops of a Territorial Bde, but the courage & quiet bearing of made of the men was of enormously, & it is worthy of comment that when early on the morning of the 9th, the two leading Coys moved to a position as a preliminary to what was expected to be an early advance under heavy shell fire, they did so to the accompaniment of the music of the mouth organ.

WAR DIARY
or
INTELLIGENCE SUMMARY
(Erase heading not required).

Army Form C. 2118.

Hour, Date, Place.	Summary of Events and Information.	Remarks and References to Appendices.
May 11th 1915	The night of the 10/11th May passed quietly, but shortly after daybreak on the 11th enemy fired a few shells at our trenches wounding 4 men of "C" Coy with shrapnel. Later in the day, he fired a few shells from a trench mortar but failed to hit the trenches. Our artillery bombarded enemy trenches at intervals during the day, & enemy retaliated, but with what effect was not known by us. Two Coys in support but D supported is orchard not sufficient billeting accommodation being at the time available. Very hot day. FD	

WAR DIARY
or
INTELLIGENCE SUMMARY

Army Form C. 21[?]

Hour, Date, Place.	Summary of Events and Information.	Remarks and References to Appendices.

April 10th 1915.

Our artillery bombarded enemy trenches at intervals during the night & p.m. the 10th Inst. Shortly after day break our men of Coy. killed by enemy sniper.

Draft of 24 men arrived to-day, 30 being sent from 10th E.R. as a reinforcement. The remaining 14 being men who had been discharged from hospital.

A. Coys relieved in trenches by 2 W. York Regt this evening. We warned to take over trenches on evening of 15th inst.

Army Form C. 2118.

WAR DIARY
or
INTELLIGENCE SUMMARY
(Erase heading not required).

Instructions regarding War Diaries and Intelligence Summaries are contained in F.S. Regs., Part II. and the Staff Manual respectively. Title pages will be prepared in manuscript.

Hour, Date, Place.	Summary of Events and Information.	Remarks and References to Appendices.
May 12th, 1915.	Weather changed. Became very wet, raining at intervals throughout the day. Artillery bombarded enemy trenches occurred at intervals during the day. Very heavy artillery fire heard most of the day from the LA BASSÉE direction. Bulletins received during afternoon announcing French successes at CARENCY, NEUVILLE ST VAAST.	

Army Form C. 2118.

WAR DIARY
or
INTELLIGENCE SUMMARY
(Erase heading not required).

Instructions regarding War Diaries and Intelligence Summaries are contained in F. S. Regs., Part II. and the Staff Manual respectively. Title pages will be prepared in manuscript.

Hour, Date, Place.	Summary of Events and Information.	Remarks and References to Appendices.
May 14th, 1915	Heavy bombardment & machine gun & rifle fire occurred at 7 a.m. this morning. Very wet night. Ground very muddy. Inspection of draft at 9 a.m. by Brigadier PINNEY. Bn then moved to Bivouac by rifle butts. C.O. Adjutant visited 9 W. YORKS REGT. those arrangements for relief by 15th.	
May 15th, 1915.	Bn then moved in billets to-day by Shepherd Billet. Weather much improved. Physical drill etc in morning. Afternoon spent in packing up kits, cleaning billets & Bivouac in preparation for taking over trenches from 9 W. YORKS REGT this evening. Coy Commanders visited trenches in morning. Arranged details of relief with Coy Commanders of 9 W. YORKS R.	

WAR DIARY
or
INTELLIGENCE SUMMARY
(Erase heading not required).

Army Form C. 2118.

Hour, Date, Place.	Summary of Events and Information.	Remarks and References to Appendices.
April 15th, 1915 MAY	Bays moved off about 4.15pm. Marched to the rendezvous agreed upon where Guides of the 3rd W.Yorks. R met them. The relief was smoothly & expeditiously carried out. At 9-40pm a message was sent to 2nd in INF. Bde reporting that relief of trenches had been accomplished.	
April 16th, 1915 MAY	There was a considerable amount of infantry & artillery fire during the night of 15/16th. But in our immediate front things were quiet. A heavy bombardment continued practically all day when the 9th & 7th Divisions are attacking near FESTUBERT. Our front very quiet in morning except	

Army Form C. 2118.

WAR DIARY
or
INTELLIGENCE SUMMARY
(Erase heading not required).

Hour, Date, Place.	Summary of Events and Information.	Remarks and References to Appendices.
	Enemy quiet.	
	After lunch visited by Brig Genl PINNEY in morning. About 3-30 pm Capt LAWRIE killed by enemy sniper in communication trench, the first officer casualty in Battalion. Shortly afterwards 2 men A Coy wounded by fire from enemy trench mortar. Later on 2 more men brought in wounded.	
May 19th, 1915.	The night 18/19th passed quietly. Shortly after day break one man D Coy killed by sniper in trenches. Weather became very hot but rained steadily most of the day. Trenches very muddy.	

WAR DIARY
or
INTELLIGENCE SUMMARY
(Erase heading not required).

Army Form C. 2118.

Hour, Date, Place.	Summary of Events and Information.	Remarks and References to Appendices.
Aug 17th 1915	Very heavy artillery fire heard nearly all day from direction of FESTUBERT. In evening Palestine bulletin announcing that two of our junior had broken enemy's line on a front of 2 miles. In some places had penetrated 1500 yds behind arrived. Rifles fitted with telescopic sights were sent to A Coy as being nearest Coy to enemy trenches. Lieut RA STOTT detailed to command M.G. section.	

WAR DIARY
or
INTELLIGENCE SUMMARY
(Erase heading not required).

Hour, Date, Place.	Summary of Events and Information.	Remarks and References to Appendices.

April 18th 1915 / The night of 17/18th passed very quietly there being practically no firing at all. Heavy rain nearly night made very bad sounds of transport moving in enemy lines everywhere. In morning Capt MURRAY reported that enemy appeared to be making to endeavour to his taught opposite A Coy the exact place was [indicated] on the map. The map together with report sent to O.C. 32nd Bty R.F.A.

6 men sent to hospital to day. Balance March B day

Army Form C. 2118.

WAR DIARY
or
INTELLIGENCE SUMMARY
(Erase heading not required).

Instructions regarding War Diaries and Intelligence Summaries are contained in F.S. Regs., Part II. and the Staff Manual respectively. Title pages will be prepared in manuscript.

Hour, Date, Place.	Summary of Events and Information.	Remarks and References to Appendices.
April 19th 1915.	The night of the 18/19th passed without incident. Heavy rain during night but stopped early in the morning. Weather very dull & misty. In afternoon enemy fired a few shells, the first two of which landed within about 50 yards from the Headquarters but none anywhere admirable of fire. The turns between the day & its very quiet all day but during evening enemy snipers were very active also his machine guns. 2 men wounded in trenches. Altogether 3 men admitted hospital to stay	

Army Form C. 2118.

WAR DIARY
or
INTELLIGENCE SUMMARY
(Erase heading not required).

Hour, Date, Place.	Summary of Events and Information.	Remarks and References to Appendices.
April 20th 1915	Early this morning enemy dropped several shells from trench mortars in Salient helped by a fog. 4 men were wounded. Two sustained injuries by falling on slippery ground. Weather became quite warm & the trenches rapidly dried. In evening enemy started dropping trench mortar bombs on Salient helped by fog, but the fact was reported to artillery who dropped 4 shells on enemy parapet which had a most specific effect on fire. Remainder of the night he was unusually quiet. 4 men admitted to hospital today.	

Army Form C. 2118.

WAR DIARY
or
INTELLIGENCE SUMMARY
(Erase heading not required).

Hour, Date, Place.	Summary of Events and Information.	Remarks and References to Appendices.
May 21st 1915	Shortly after daybreak to-day Captain BOYD wounded. Later in the morning 2 men were wounded. A very heavy storm occurred in the morning & the trenches soon became a sea of mud. Coy Commanders of 2nd Sn visited the trenches with preparatory to taking over in the evening. Nothing of note occurred during the day. At night Bn was relieved by the 2nd Co S.co RIF. Relief completed about 10.15pm when Bn moved into Barracks in RUE BACQUEROT. B & D Coys in billets about 600 yds behind trenches Hqrs in close support	

WAR DIARY
or
INTELLIGENCE SUMMARY
(Erase heading not required).

Army Form C. 2118.

Hour, Date, Place.	Summary of Events and Information.	Remarks and References to Appendices.
May August 22nd 1915	4 men admitted hospital to-day. Day spent in cleaning up, inspection of clothing equipment etc. Coys visited Divisional Baths at SAILLY Very hot day	
May August 23rd 1915	4 men admitted 1 man R.A.M.C. (stores) admitted hospital to day then G.S.O. Stove Coys went for a run before breakfast R.C. & Presbyterian services at 8½ & 9½" a.m" Working party of 100 men furnished a Pty Pr for work under 1st Home Counties R.E.	

Army Form C. 2118.

WAR DIARY
or
INTELLIGENCE SUMMARY
(Erase heading not required).

Hour, Date, Places.	Summary of Events and Information.	Remarks and References to Appendices.
April 24th May 24th, 1915.	1 Man admitted to hospital to-day. Very hot day. Boys went for a run before breakfast. After breakfast, all Coys went for a route march about 7 miles working party of 100 men furnished for work under R.E.	
May 25th, 1915.	3 men admitted to hospital to-day. Stopping hot. Programme of work same as yesterday. Working party of 50 men furnished for work under R.E.	

WAR DIARY
or
INTELLIGENCE SUMMARY

Army Form C. 2118.

Hour, Date, Place.	Summary of Events and Information.	Remarks and References to Appendices.
May 26th 1915.	4 men admitted Hospital to-day. In moving Coys went for a run. After breakfast enemy suddenly shelled billets B Coy about 9 pm. Their firing unsatisfactorily accurate as they fired a salvo of 4 shells the 3rd & 4 dropping in the billets. At the time this started, the men who had been feeding outside, were commencing to get their rifles & equipment out of the billets for parade, but the 3rd shell was right in the horses & the men had	

Shake for cover.) There were no casualties but
6.3 rifles & 4 sets of equipment were burnt
together with the rats. & all the Coy officers
The enemy shelled this place surrounding
points fairly steadily most of the morning but
was necessary to keep the men in dugouts Mainly
during that time.
Indents were forwarded to Ordnance Rifles &
musts of equipment were received that night
first issue of short rifles received to-day.
Working party of 150 men furnished to-night
for works under R.E.

WAR DIARY
or
INTELLIGENCE SUMMARY
(Erase heading not required).

Army Form C. 2118.

Hour, Date, Place.	Summary of Events and Information.	Remarks and References to Appendices.
May 24th	4 men admitted to hospital to-day. One of them being wounded. Day spent mostly in cleaning up billets. Coys went for a short march. In the evening Batt. relieved 2/ Sco. Rifles in F. Lines. Relief commenced at 6.30 pm & was complete by 10 pm. One man of "B" Coy wounded by stray bullet behind trench headquarters.	

Army Form C. 2118.

WAR DIARY
or
INTELLIGENCE SUMMARY
(Erase heading not required).

Instructions regarding War Diaries and Intelligence Summaries are contained in F.S. Regs., Part II. and the Staff Manual respectively. Title pages will be prepared in manuscript.

Hour, Date, Place.	Summary of Events and Information.	Remarks and References to Appendices.
May 28th 1915	The night of the 27/28th passed quietly. There was a burst of rapid fire about 11-30 pm. mostly from our own lines. Pte A. Thouin taught in the wheel desultory firing. Nothing of incident occurred very quiet all day. 3 men wounded (but slightly) & one man admitted to hospital with illness. Pte P. Phelan Chevaux de Frize wire entanglements put out during the night	
May 29th 1915	Nothing of incident occurred during the night of the 28/29 th. The morning passed quietly. At about 12-30 pm Enemy shelled Bn HQ. Vicinity heavily until 4-45 pm. There were no casualties. Pte Stokes was wounded in the	

H.Q.O.
900. 7-14.

WAR DIARY
or
INTELLIGENCE SUMMARY.
(Erase heading not required.)

Army Form C. 2118.

Hour, Date, Place	Summary of Events and Information	Remarks and references to Appendices

field where the dug outs were situated. One shell dropped within 3yds of the dug out when the Sgt Major was. It soon became obvious that the dug outs were in the line of fire, & a move was made to some deep shelbrow trenches about 50yds away, where a Sharpshooter Security was kept.

During the evening 2nd Lt J.S. HARDIE was severely wounded whilst in command of a reconnoitring patrol. He was admitted to 24th Field Ambulance

WAR DIARY
or
INTELLIGENCE SUMMARY

Army Form C. 2118.

Hour, Date, Place	Summary of Events and Information	Remarks and references to Appendices
May 30th, 1915.	The night of 29/30th May passed quietly except for this incident described in yesterday's diary. The early morning was enlivened by the enemy shouting epithets that the enemy shouted across his parapet. The enemy was astonished by no reply from our front as was evidenced by his remark. Enemy was observed the very day working in his trenches all day. About 5pm enemy shifted salient of trench held by A Coy for about 45 minutes wounding Capt Murray and five men. None of them seriously hurt, the wounds being only flesh ones.	

WAR DIARY or INTELLIGENCE SUMMARY.
(Erase heading not required.)

Army Form C. 2118.

Hour, Date, Place	Summary of Events and Information	Remarks and references to Appendices
	Later on the evening one man killed in the trenches by a rifle bullet. Total no of admissions to hospital to-day Capt Murray & five men	
May 31st 1915	Nothing of interest occurred during the night. The 31st May the enemy made no effort to interfere with the working party repairing the breach in the parapet. In the evening "A" Coy the 5th men the frontage of "B" & "C" Coys in E lines & the two Coys were relieved by 2/ W YORKS R. Very quiet day. 3 men admitted hospital to day	Casualties K 1 + 4 W 2 + 25 M. 9 K 1 + 4 W 2 + 75 Sick no = 3 + 75

51ST DIVISION
154TH INFY BDE

1-6TH BN SCOTTISH RIFLES
~~MAR~~ ~~JUNE 1915~~ ~~FEB 1916~~
JUN 1915 TO MAY 1916

AMALGAMATED
WITH 5 BN.
33 Div 19 Bde

Confidential

War Diary
of
1/6th Scottish Rifles

From 1st June 1915 To 30th June 1915

Vol I

Hour, Date, Place.	Summary of Events and Information.	Remarks and References to Appendices.
June 1st 1915	Very quiet during the day. At 3.15 P.M. in the morning enemy dropped a few shells into a house at FAVOISART Crossroads where a few men were billeted. Nowhere doing any damage. About 3 p.m. H.H a message came announcing that the Bn had been transferred to 152nd Brigade of the Highland Division. In the evening the Bn was relieved in trenches by 21 S.O.S & the Bn & men into billets vacated by the 21 S.O.S →	

WAR DIARY
or
INTELLIGENCE SUMMARY

Army Form C. 2118.

Hour, Date, Place.	Summary of Events and Information.	Remarks and References to Appendices.
June 2nd 1915	The night after stand had passed is pilots rested. Early in the afternoon a message was received to the effect that the Sqn was branch at 3pm from the 154th Sqdn of the 51st (Highland) Division. The Sqn left at 3pm. Genl DAVIS being the 8th Division, & Brigad PINNEY accompanied the Sqn. The truth of 5th Division area. The Sqn arrived at its destination at Le CORNET MALO, about 4 kilometres N of BÉTHUNE, previous to kick.	

WAR DIARY
or
INTELLIGENCE SUMMARY.
(Erase heading not required.)

Army Form C. 2118.

Hour, Date, Place	Summary of Events and Information	Remarks and references to Appendices
	Day is different — being duty rewarded. The 154th Bde of the "Highland Division" is reinforced by 3 English Bns, this Bn being the only Scottish one in the Brigade. 2nd Lt MACDONALD & one man were admitted to hospital to day.	
June 23rd 1915	For the night of 22/23rd June passed quietly but uncomfortably for the Batt H.Q. staff. The only accommodation is the the farm allotted being one rather dingy room, yet we	

WAR DIARY
or
INTELLIGENCE SUMMARY.

(Erase heading not required.)

Army Form C. 2118.

Hour, Date, Place	Summary of Events and Information	Remarks and references to Appendices

Necessary for every Officer with the exception of the C.O. to Bivouac.
The day was spent quietly. Roll Calls had a Rattling Parade in the morning.
The AIRE – LA BASSEE Canal Between being quite close to the Bivouac.
In the afternoon the 1/4 Q.L. moved to a new short bivouac from our present place (the 15th Inf-de Camp outside) to Tuesday night (1 tent) in now Divisional Reserve.

WAR DIARY
or
INTELLIGENCE SUMMARY.
(Erase heading not required.)

Army Form C. 2118.

Instructions regarding War Diaries and Intelligence Summaries are contained in F.S. Regs., Part II and the Staff Manual respectively. Title pages will be prepared in manuscript.

Hour, Date, Place	Summary of Events and Information	Remarks and references to Appendices
June 2nd 1915	Very hot day. Batt went for a route march of about 5 miles. In the afternoon bathing parades were held.	
June 3rd 1915	Battment for a route march of about 6 miles. In the afternoon C.O. & Adjutant went to a conference at Bde HQrs regarding the taking over of trenches from 153rd Bde on the 8th. 3 men admitted to hospital to-day.	

WAR DIARY
or
INTELLIGENCE SUMMARY.
(Erase heading not required.)

Army Form C. 2118.

Hour, Date, Place	Summary of Events and Information	Remarks and references to Appendices
Trenches N/ps June 5th – 11th 1915	Very hot day. Coy Commanders & B.M.D. Coy N.C. Officer visited trenches to be taken over the Battalion. In the afternoon Batt Cpl Pilots proceeded to cross roads at LE TOURET where it was met by guides from 1/7th Black Watch & 1/4 to Gordon Highlanders. The relief was rather complicated owing to the fact that the Fire & Support trenches were taken over from 1/7 to B.W. & the Reserve Trenches from 1/4 to Gordon Highlanders.	

WAR DIARY
or
INTELLIGENCE SUMMARY.
(Erase heading not required.)

Army Form C. 2118.

Hour, Date, Place	Summary of Events and Information	Remarks and references to Appendices

To add further to the diff'culties the only means of communication was a long narrow, very indifferent communication trench, through which the battalion going into the line coming out of the trenches had to pass.

The fire trenches were also very narrow but there was great diff'culty in passing along the tunnel B & D Coys both over the fire trenches & A & C the reserve.

Army Form C. 2118.

WAR DIARY
or
INTELLIGENCE SUMMARY.
(Erase heading not required.)

Instructions regarding War Diaries and Intelligence Summaries are contained in F.S. Regs., Part II. and the Staff Manual respectively. Title pages will be prepared in manuscript.

Hour, Date, Place	Summary of Events and Information	Remarks and references to Appendices
	The relief was a very slow tedious business & was due principally to the bad communications, shortly to the inexperience of the 3 Bns, neither of which had had the advantage of being associated with regular troops & learning a methodical way of carrying out trench relief. The relief which commenced at 9pm was ultimately completed at 7-30pm on the morning of the 9th.	

WAR DIARY
or
INTELLIGENCE SUMMARY.
(Erase heading not required.)

Army Form C. 2118.

Hour, Date, Place	Summary of Events and Information	Remarks and references to Appendices

The Coy remained in the trenches until relieved on the night of the 9th.

During that period there was incessant artillery fire by high explosive almost without cessation. The enemy raking party each day & occasionally at night.

Only on one occasion were our trenches badly shelled, when both our own artillery & the enemy selected B Coy in this trench as their target.

Fortunately the casualties were slight, 2nd Lt DAVIE & 3 men

WAR DIARY
or
INTELLIGENCE SUMMARY.
(Erase heading not required.)

Army Form C. 2118.

Hour, Date, Place	Summary of Events and Information	Remarks and references to Appendices

being wounded.
The reserve trenches were only shelled by
our own artillery, also luckily without
damage.
As these trenches were some 1000 yds behind
the fire trench, it is hard to realize why
they were selected as a Target, but it was
presumably due either to indifferent
laying or to defective ammunition.
The ration & water supply to the fire trenches
took a great deal of time every night

the offs either of supply were accentuated by the fact that both of the reserve Coys were on duty every night as a working party under the supervision of the R.E.

Another means of communication was discovered to the support trench, rather this Batt was relieved on the night of the 9/10th June, the relief thus carried out fairly expeditiously, the relief was completed soon after midnight. The Bn then went into billets near

WAR DIARY
or
INTELLIGENCE SUMMARY.
(Erase heading not required.)

Army Form C. 2118.

Hour, Date, Place	Summary of Events and Information	Remarks and references to Appendices
	LE TOURET which were reached between 1-30am & 2am on the 15th. Total casualties during this period 1 Officer & 5 men wounded.	
June 10th	Coys spent the afternoon cleaning up billets, most of which were indescribably filthy when entered into. Latrines seemed to have been unknown in the Billet, Pvs to Billet was there a refuse or souk pit.	

WAR DIARY
or
INTELLIGENCE SUMMARY.
(Erase heading not required.)

Army Form C. 2118.

Hour, Date, Place	Summary of Events and Information	Remarks and references to Appendices
	In the afternoon enemy fired a few shells at long range, one man of transport section was wounded, also 1 mule & 1 horse. Very heavy thunderstorm early the morning. Some of the Platoons were flooded out. Working party of 100 men found by night 7.D.	
June 11th 1915.	Very heavy thunderstorm early in. Very heavy rain during the night & country very muddy. Coy paraded Physical in the morning. Coy paraded Physical	

WAR DIARY
INTELLIGENCE SUMMARY

Summary of Events and Information

1.25 Orders shell arrived RE.
In the afternoon orders received for a
working party of 312 men for work in the
trenches during the night of 9th/10th/12th.
Later on news received that 153 rd & 54th
was relieving the 2 Bn of the 7 & 8th Brigades
in the trenches. Enquiry on enquiry being
made from Bn H.Q. as to the disposal
of the 2 M. guns per charge of the Bn
which had been sent to 1/5th Liverpool Regt.
The M.G. Officer was informed that
these guns were [to] be taken [by] the trenches

Army Form C. 2118.

WAR DIARY
or
INTELLIGENCE SUMMARY
(Erase heading not required.)

Instructions regarding War Diaries and Intelligence Summaries are contained in F.S. Regs., Part II and the Staff Manual respectively. Title pages will be prepared in manuscript.

Hour, Date, Place	Summary of Events and Information	Remarks and references to Appendices
	handed over to the 8th the relieving Bn of the 13th Bde. About 9 p.m. an urgent message was received that the two Coys of the Bn withdrawn. The M.G. Officer turned out his section at once & the M.G.s taken were [illegible] harnessed up. The section proceeded to the trenches [illegible] a distance of about 3 miles. After some considerable delay a message was received from OC H.Q. stating	

WAR DIARY
or
INTELLIGENCE SUMMARY

Army Form C. 2118.

Hour, Date, Place	Summary of Events and Information	Remarks and references to Appendices
	that the guns should be I, before withdrawn & accordingly the O.C. Section then returned to their Billets having lasted some hours & well earned rest after a rather trying 2 days in the trenches 5 men admitted to hospital to-day	
June 15th 1915	A message received early this morning stating that the Bn was under the orders of the G.O.C. 153rd W INF BDE until further orders. Later on an order was received from 153rd W INF BDE that the Battalion was to proceed from Billets near LE TOURET	

WAR DIARY
or
INTELLIGENCE SUMMARY.
(Erase heading not required.)

Army Form C. 2118.

Hour, Date, Place	Summary of Events and Information	Remarks and references to Appendices
	To billets about LE CORNET MALO in the Course of the afternoon. In accordance with these orders the Bn moved to the billets allotted which were reached between 3-30 + 4 p.m. Shortly after 9 p.m. an order was received from 152td INF Bde that C.O. Adjutant + Coy Cmdrs were to attend at BdeHQrs at 9.a.m tomorrow. Men admitted to hospital to-day	

WAR DIARY
INTELLIGENCE SUMMARY

Army Form C. 2118

Place	Date	Hour	Summary of Events and Information	Remarks and references to Appendices
Le CORNET MALO	13th June		At G.C.H. O.C., Adj, Int, & Coy Commanders attended the conference at Brigade Head Quarters reported to in yesterday's diary. Before the conference Bryn General R. Bannatyne-Allason commanding the 55th Division addressed those present, who included all the O.C.'s & Adjutants of the Brigade, i.e. 1/4th King's Own (Royal Lancaster) Reg., 1/6th King's Liverpool Reg., 1/5th Seaforth Rifles, & 1/4th & 1/4th West Lancashire Reg. He informed the Col. the Brigade had been selected to make an attack on the enemy & 16th W.Lt. rehearses his employee in the revert. At the experience this O.C. Coy S.O. 1 upon Div - explained that a very experienced artillery preparation wite attack would be made starting from today & that in addition to our own 8 how & 14 Heavy 75 M.L. guns & some heavy trench Mr. Into Brigade line w Howitzer the next over his attack will & upon the	

1875 Wt. W593/826 1,000,000 4/15 J.B.C. & A. A.D.S.S./Forms/C. 2118.

WAR DIARY
or
INTELLIGENCE SUMMARY
(Erase heading not required.)

Army Form C. 2118

Place	Date	Hour	Summary of Events and Information	Remarks and references to Appendices
	15th June 1915		Attack was to be launched at 6 p.m. on the evening of the 15th inst. The troops I commanded being under the orders of the 6th Div. Ryde & the 4th Gds had been; were Bttns acting as covering on the frontage of a Return erect with the hostile power on the right. The Scottish Ryde in the left. The night Bttn were chiefly to be 2nd frontage woven the 200 yds. The envelopes troops were carry on the advance by platoons into the positions were captured from Seap Head L.8, the objective being a general seap lane chiefly opposite - the Kings Own to be in support, & the Kings & Liverpool Reg. in reserve at LE TOURET a matter of some 3 or 4 miles back - The envelope Batts were to take over the trenches in front of FESTUBERT trenches held by the 7th Div. in wonencies on the night of the 5-15th & the [illegible] Div. to hold their night - there Div. to hits & warned	

1875. Wt. W593/826 1,000,000 4/15 J.B.C. & A. A.D.S.S./Forms/C. 2118.

WAR DIARY
or
INTELLIGENCE SUMMARY
(Erase heading not required.)

Army Form C. 2118

Place	Date	Hour	Summary of Events and Information	Remarks and references to Appendices
	13 June 1915		Ambulance well at the stone barn. Revd. Col. C.F. O'Kane C.M.S. Cavalry 1st Brigade Shaws (7th Div), who was present, gave some medical suggestions as to details. At home we carried out in the usual way but in creating the Battalion & being relieved by in line 2 Coys each up to 6th D.7th Norse Hghldrs S. Bay. Relieving the front trench, D – Sudbutt, D.A.D.e in reserve. About midnight 2/Lieut. D.S. COLVILLE, whose unit, the sentries on a advanced post held by A Coy, was wounded in the lower by a stray shrapnel.	
FESTUBERT	14 June 1915		A busy day. We spent whatever time we could in getting information. However events enabled us to settle that we went right & to stay. Important steps we received a certain amount of attention in the trenches but from the sum of the enemy shells, D.T.G. bombed in the front trench was	

WAR DIARY or INTELLIGENCE SUMMARY

Army Form C. 2118

Place	Date	Hour	Summary of Events and Information	Remarks and references to Appendices
FESTUBERT	June 14th 1915		Comparatively calm day. There were a few men wounded in the trenches, but none very seriously. 2/Lieut. C.G. MACDONALD who was in hospital reported for duty this forenoon; he has not been well, but having heard of the attack, moved up from young & was Trench again. [N.B. He served 0 (serving?) the combat with previous coy.) Capt. J. LUSK, Gen. Staff Officer, also called to have a look around in place of his own 2/Lieut. COLVILLE, wounded yesterday. In view of the bad weather, his request here to be repeated — The Battalion was in the high level shields at the moment of engaging the enemy.	

WAR DIARY or INTELLIGENCE SUMMARY

Army Form C. 2118

Place	Date	Hour	Summary of Events and Information	Remarks and references to Appendices
FESTUBERT	14th June 1915		In the course of the evening the 4th King's Own moved into the Reserve Trenches in support to Battalion. A & C Coys moved up by night to the fire trench & our front within 5 of our own front line. During the evening the travel duckboards along our front line were broken — these bridges were needed to be put onto our own wire connecting us up to Speewell trench dug out, & materials arrived for this work came here & good deal of wire fixing & methodical arrangements in the trench [?] made. Remainder pers civilian line sentinelled.	
do.	15th June 1915		In the morning Brig Genl W.J.S. Murray, D the day Murray bringing it in the morning. His visits [?] & Indian Service Chg 9 visits / hrs.	

WAR DIARY
or
INTELLIGENCE SUMMARY

Army Form C. 2118

Place	Date	Hour	Summary of Events and Information	Remarks and references to Appendices
FESTUBERT.	15th June 1915		S/Lieut. hatching on the L.H. of the WORKS – The artillery on both sides were active, & a good deal of hostile fire was directed on the fire & support trenches – During the burst of fire D Coy in the support trench sustained 16 casualties, & a number of men in A & C Coys in the front were dealt with during the day. About 3 p.m. 2/Lieut. A.G.E. HILL (A Coy) was severely wounded in the thumb. A message was received from the 154th Bde that the precaution measures the seemed to in Tarnier bombardment indicated hoped to during the attack.— From 5.30 p.m. 5.45 p.m. Heavy bombardment of enemy front trench. — 5.55 to 6.3 Slackened in ..do.. — 6.3 to 6.6 a height of 100 yards forward. — 6.6 to 6.21 Bombardment of enemy 2nd line trenches.	

Place	Date	Hour	Summary of Events and Information	Remarks and references to Appendices
FESTUBERT	15·14 June 15·15		From 6.21 A.m. heavy bombardment of RUE D'ENFER 90. No details were given but subsequent action yet Since 9 it was announced they were no forming the recent trenches itself, in men to formerly the recent barrage with difficulty. O 15 the men. The Brigade then sent also ordered Ncol. The heavy Artillery who to all were at 5·57 p.m. sorted to begin in return to the enemy trench before the front lift. By the first hour haul (6·30 p.m.) the bombardment in our side had become very heavy & on the trench & that of the enemy support a great deal of damage. The survivors between enemy received & grew heavy shell & huge volumes up out of stones were cut stones. Shown up. All wires	

Place	Date	Hour	Summary of Events and Information	Remarks and references to Appendices
FESTUBERT	15th & 16th 1915		Had been synchronised with Army time hourly during the day & the hourly Watson of A Coy & the Battalion, emphatically 2/Lieut. C.S. MACDONALD, together with the hourly Watson gth 1/14 London Regt Reserve Regt. Imperialle Ireland exactly at 5.57 p.m. Several Coys in the assault viz. A, C, D & B. The Battalion Bombers had assembled at the first 1000m over, & two machine guns positioned at the rear of A Coy on frontage believed to be about 100 yards to the left up to his between L8 & the Army Sap. D the chicken as to be erected in about 20 yards - the whirled & crawled to the first lot in the first line. The deep dited, repaired to above, had to be crossed before the enemy trench was reached - C & D Coys followed close on the heels of A Coy; & Major SHAW crossed with the Dt. Hy Coy; the commanding Officer & a certain new came L. 8 with B Coy as Battalion Reserve. Shortly after the heavy Watson	

WAR DIARY
or
INTELLIGENCE SUMMARY

Army Form C. 2118

Place	Date	Hour	Summary of Events and Information	Remarks and references to Appendices
FESTUBERT	15th June 1915		Left our Trench the whole of our Trench, L & D the Surrendered it. The German Trench were absolutely delayed will have one Artillery of all sizes, included 9 in Triple 9 1st Trench and Sets had were badly damaged; in fact the 5up was intended by the two German Trenches however by Everetts Suh by the two leading Coy's. It was arrived that the Reserve Coy was to establish it. We seemed to get forward, however with the P.O.D. however, wherever but we were in unity in Situation D. with a house was said to be still remain by the enemy, the 9 the hurry then Salient, man of Taken at the houses up the bayonet. A artill shewed when after it was stated that he had witnessed a number of charges by infantry since the was on moved, but he had never seen one carried out with such vin & resolution	

WAR DIARY
or
INTELLIGENCE SUMMARY

(Erase heading not required.)

Army Form C. 2118

Place	Date	Hour	Summary of Events and Information	Remarks and references to Appendices
FESTUBERT	16th June 1915		It was intensely splendid to see it snow & terrific fire — Our artillery had completely cut the wire in front of the enemy Schick, but a little to the left past the wire was here when in fact 9 men yet were held in attempts to cut it & force a way through — Those men who went through were the first to enter it — which in the bridge were shot at & clothed by the hurts artillery at a very early stage yet we could represent trench was found the weapons in some shelters, but it's german was chased out by bombs & the bayonet — As we pushed forward up the German trench a number to the enemy took refuge in their shelters & others more I heard to the advancing bombers to show them, but the bombers remembered FROMELLES on 9th MAY, & the work of our 2nd / Battn at NEUVE CHAPPELLE, & gave no quarter — Before we call the enemy were completely driven out of the Schick, & we have captured the second line — At this point their resistance became more	

1875 Wt. W593/826 1,000,000 4/15 J.B.C. & A. A.D.S.S./Forms/C. 2118.

WAR DIARY
or
INTELLIGENCE SUMMARY

(Erase heading not required.)

Army Form C. 2118

Place	Date	Hour	Summary of Events and Information	Remarks and references to Appendices
FESTUBERT	June 15 15		determined & strong reinforcements were seen coming up the rise in the ground to their support — he had lost very heavily. By this time 9 only 3 Officers were left; 3 wounded were absolutely unnerving but no more arrived. The remains of the Batln: Coy. then seemed to hang on — The fire of the enemy's machine guns & rifles was heavy he being in our left flank. He was seriously threatened by their bombers — In spite of all however the Batln: held the ground won — As the Batln: & the King's Lpool were the only troops who had got through, our flanks were much exposed, the attack by right brigade had not been entirely successful — The position was in consequence returning in their own trench. — The Batln: however having received no orders kept their ground & held staunch[ly]	

Army Form C. 2118

WAR DIARY
or
INTELLIGENCE SUMMARY
(Erase heading not required.)

Instructions regarding War Diaries and Intelligence Summaries are contained in F. S. Regs., Part II. and the Staff Manual respectively. Title Pages will be prepared in manuscript.

Place	Date	Hour	Summary of Events and Information	Remarks and references to Appendices
FESTUBERT	15/16 June 1915		before 10 a.m. until morning of the 16th June, when they received an order to retire — She withdrawal was expected in a lu o St Maine work & orderly manner, but important defs in any case when were sustained before our trench was reached —	

WAR DIARY
or
INTELLIGENCE SUMMARY.
(Erase heading not required.)

Army Form C. 2118.

Hour, Date, Place	Summary of Events and Information	Remarks and references to Appendices
Night of 15/16th June.	At 10pm Quartermaster & Transport Officer reached village of FESTUBERT with two mule water carts, 50 empty dixies, a ration of rum in jars and a carrying party of 25 men furnished from transport section personnel. These men were divided into five parties under the four Company Quartermaster Sergeants & the Sergeant tailor. The 50 dixies were filled with water from the carts & the five parties carried them down road to support trench. A good interval was kept between parties as the road was being shelled, & trench was reached about 10.45pm. The Medical Officer was particularly glad to get this water as his supply was exhausted.	

WAR DIARY
or
INTELLIGENCE SUMMARY

Army Form C. 2118.

Hour, Date, Place	Summary of Events and Information	Remarks and references to Appendices
Wednesday 16th June	The Regimental First Aid Post meanwhile which opened by 5pm and which it might have been supposed it could not have withstood a direct hit. In this shelter the Medical Officer and his Staff were passing through a very strenuous time & anxious and trying work under conditions of exceedingly great difficulty, and had already passed a large number of cases through their hands. The Adjutant now returned to FESTUBERT & took charge of Transport while Transport Officer went out to the fire trench. About midnight 2/Lieut A.C. STEWART passed down the communication trench towards the aid post wounded, but quite able to walk. By this time the 1/8th Liverpool Regiment were in occupation of the fire trench	

WAR DIARY
or
INTELLIGENCE SUMMARY.
(Erase heading not required.)

Army Form C. 2118.

Hour, Date, Place	Summary of Events and Information	Remarks and references to Appendices
	and the men of the 6 Scottish Rifles who had come back into the fire trench over the parapet were scattered up and down the trench so that an effort was made to arrange that the 1/8th Royal Scots Regt. should close in towards the right so as to permit the 6th Cameron Rifles to re-organize in a section of trench by themselves. It was a matter of some difficulty to collect them as those seemed to be very few NCO's left and of the officers who took part in the attack the only ones available then were Lieut Ralston Lieut Campbell and Lieut Hay (who has been leading the Brigade Bombers). While the men were passing along the fire trench towards the left two came carrying 2/Lieut WISHART in a waterproof sheet. He was very pale from loss of blood and although he took some water from a water bottle, it is	

WAR DIARY
or
INTELLIGENCE SUMMARY.
(Erase heading not required.)

Army Form C. 2118.

Hour, Date, Place	Summary of Events and Information	Remarks and references to Appendices
	doubtful if he recognised anyone. It was difficult to prevent men from going down communication trench on some pretext or other and about 3 am when the majority of those left in fire trench had been got to further an effort was made to get into telephone communication with the Brigade to ask for fresh orders. The wires between the Brigade Headqrs and support trench had all been cut by the shelling and it was only possible to speak to the Cotter trench from which a major of the 14th Royal Lancashire Regt. (Kirk's own) spoke and said that a message has been received from the Brigade to the effect that the 6th Scottish Rifles were to withdraw to support trench and reform there. By degrees this was done under a good deal	

WAR DIARY
or
INTELLIGENCE SUMMARY.
(Erase heading not required.)

Army Form C. 2118.

Hour, Date, Place	Summary of Events and Information	Remarks and references to Appendices

shell fire which rendered the work of our stretcher bearers very difficult. At many parts of the communication trench the ordinary stretcher could not be used so that it had to be abandoned and a carrier improvised from a waterproof sheet instead. On arrival at Support trench it was found that the following message apparently written at 4.39 am was waiting for the Battalion:— B.M. 507 16th (day of month) As many officers and men of 1st Battalion as can be collected should be taken back to LE TOURET where arrangements are being made for food and not AAA As two Battalions are remaining as trench garrison you should not crowd trenches more by waiting AAA So soon as small parties are collected they should start at once for LE TOURET." Time 4.37 am (Signed) G.D. Bruce, Major from 154 Inf. Brig.

No 929 Sergt T. HILLHOUSE of "B" Coy had died of wounds at the Aid Post during the night and was buried in a grave dug immediately in rear of the support trench
Captain J.C. McLEAN was resting in a "dug out". He was obviously suffering from very severe shock and seemed not to recognise any one. He was carried off on a stretcher. What remained of each Company was marches off from the support trench but, remaining N.C.Os being the By 6am all were clear of the trench, the last above being the remaining officers of the Battalion, namely Major J.L. London, RAMC, Lieut D. Ralston, Lieut T.H. Campbell, the transport officer & Sergt. Major W. Baldock. Lieut J.C.E. Hay has returned to Brigade Headqrs at an earlier hour in the morning to report regarding Brigade Bombing operations etc.
The books at Regt. Aid Post showed that between 6 pm on 15th and 6am on 16th the names of 10 officers and 203 NCOs and men has been recorded as having passed through the hands of the medical Staff. There were numerous other cases however whose names it was

not possible to obtain a record of the time. The invaluable services rendered by the Medical Officer during this trying trip up to period can better be imagined than described, as he was very ably assisted in his work by Corporal R. WHYTHAM, RAMC(T).

The Medical Officer walked towards LE TOURET via Brigade Headquarters and there reported to Brigadier General HIBBERT as much as was known of the night's operation and the approximate losses sustained. The General expressed his satisfaction that the Battn. had done so well in the attack and his extreme regret for the loss of life involved. There seemed to be no satisfactory explanation why the Battalion was not supported on the flanks as it should have been.

At LE TOURET, A field kitchen chosen opposite to one where the Transport were parked; the travelling kitchens has been drawn alongside by the Quartermaster and there the Companies Lattices out had a hot meal and rest. Fortunately the day was fine.

WAR DIARY
or
INTELLIGENCE SUMMARY

(Erase heading not required.)

Army Form C. 2118

Place	Date	Hour	Summary of Events and Information	Remarks and references to Appendices
			About 9 am a Car drew up at Kapus with some members of the Divisional Staff who picked up Lieuts. Ralph & Campbell and took them off to report their experiences to the Divisional General.	
			At 11.30 am Roll call was held. Engagement and of those who took part in the Engagement the following numbers answered their name in each Company. "A" Coy. 60; "B" Coy. 99; "C" Coy. 97; "D" Coy. 101; Total 357 As far as could be ascertained at that time the following numbers of each Company had gone into trenches on the night of 13/14 June "A" Coy. 161; "B" Coy. 180; "C" Coy. 174; "D" Coy. 190; Total 705 There had been 2 "other ranks" casualties on 13th and 2 on 14th. [?] the number killed accounted for as 701,- so that apparently the casualties of other ranks amounted to 344 due to the engagement of 15/16th June. It was thought	

WAR DIARY

or

INTELLIGENCE SUMMARY

(Erase heading not required.)

Army Form C. 2118

Place	Date	Hour	Summary of Events and Information	Remarks and references to Appendices

			known that it was quite probable that some others might report themselves later. Of the 21 officers (excluding medical officer) who took part in the action on the night of 15/16th June only 3 remained fit for duty namely Lieut. D. RALSTON (machine gun officer), Lieut J.C.E. HAY and Lieut T.H. CAMPBELL
			
			Evidence was all too abundant that the following Officers had been killed while leading their commands
			
			    Major D. P. SHAW (2nd in Command)
			    Captain C. J. C. MURRAY
			    Captain J. BROWN
			    Lieutenant P. H. KEITH
			    2nd Lieutenant J. B. WILSON
			    2nd Lieutenant C. G. MACDONALD
			    2nd Lieutenant G. McC. KENNEDY.	

Army Form C. 2118

WAR DIARY
or
INTELLIGENCE SUMMARY
(Erase heading not required.)

Instructions regarding War Diaries and Intelligence Summaries are contained in F.S. Regs., Part II. and the Staff Manual respectively. Title Pages will be prepared in manuscript.

Place	Date	Hour	Summary of Events and Information	Remarks and references to Appendices
			The following Officers has been wounded :—	
			Lieut Colonel N. MARTIN KAY T.D., Commanding	
			Captain F.G.W. DRAFFEN Adjutant	
			Major N.S. McKENZIE	
			Lieutenant J.G. LOGAN	
			2nd Lieutenant A.C. STEWART	
			2nd Lieutenant A.G.E. HILL	
			2nd Lieutenant A.W. BROWN	
			2nd Lieutenant W.R. WISHART	
			Of these the most seriously wounded were 2/Lieutenant W.R. WISHART and 2nd Lieutenant A.G.E. HILL	
			The following Officers although not actually struck by shell or bullet were suffering from very severe shock.	
			Captain J.C. McLEAN.	
			Captain J.H. KEITH	
			2/Lieutenant W. CAPES	

WAR DIARY
or
INTELLIGENCE SUMMARY
(Erase heading not required.)

All wounded Officers were taken to the 1/2nd Highland Field Ambulance at LOCON, and after being kept there for varying short periods were sent on to No 4 Casualty Clearing Station at LILLERS. Late

Ammony was received from 154th Inf. Bde. that the Battn were much with its transport to the billets which it formerly occupied in LE CORNET MALO and would there be under the orders of 153rd Inf. Bde.

The Battalion accordingly marched off in the later part of the afternoon followed by the transport. The column was sadly reduced in length, but the spirit of the men was wonderful notwithstanding the exceedingly trying experiences through which they had so recently come.

WAR DIARY
or
INTELLIGENCE SUMMARY
(Erase heading not required.)

Army Form C. 2118

LE CORNET MALO was reached in the evening and Bill of-
Wort allotted to Companies as formerly occupied by them.
The trenching in State reported to 153rd Inf Bde were as
follows:-
  Officers   5
  Other ranks   437 } inclusive attacks
         Total 442

That night an attack was the made on the same
Ground by 1/8th (Irish) King's Liverpool Rgt. preceded by the
heavy artillery bombardment. This renewed it impossible
that any attempt could be made that night to bring in any
wounded who might still be lying out.

Army Form C. 2118

WAR DIARY
or
INTELLIGENCE SUMMARY
(Erase heading not required.)

Place	Date	Hour	Summary of Events and Information	Remarks and references to Appendices
	Thursday 17 June		In the morning a thorough inspection by Companies of arms, equipment and clothing was made and all deficiencies have noted and reported. It was felt that since on the previous night it had been impossible to evacuate any of the wounded who might still need help, something must be done on this night, and so anyway no such effort on behalf of the wounded not left to take a party of volunteers under an officer up to the trenches at night to make some attempt. Permission was granted. There was no lack of volunteers, and 10 NCOs and men were chosen from each Company and 10 from Transport Section. These were furnished with rations and carried full water bottles and an additional bread ration which	In afternoon Capt. A.G. Graham proceeded to Brigade H.Q. & took Command of Battalion.

Lieut. J.J.C. WILSON also returned from visit to Royal Flying Corps. |

1875 Wt. W593/826 1,000,000 4/15 J.B.C. & A. A.D.S.S./Forms/C. 2118.

WAR DIARY
or
INTELLIGENCE SUMMARY

(Erase heading not required.)

Army Form C. 2118

Place	Date	Hour	Summary of Events and Information	Remarks and references to Appendices
			It was thought might prove useful. This party of S.D., accompanied by Lieut. D. RALSTON, Lieut. J.C.F. HAY, and Capt. J. LUSK set out for the trenches about 6pm a distance of over 8 miles. On the way a halt was made near LOCON at Brigade Headrs and instructions were received from General Hibbert that before the parts actually went down to trenches his Compliments were to be presented to General Campbell Comdg. 153rd Inf. Bde who were occupying the fire trench, and his permission was to be obtained before proceeding further. At about 9pm Head qrs of 153rd Inf Bde. were reached at the farm with moto round it. General Campbell was seen and his sanction requested. He said he had no objection to the attempt being made provided it did not	

WAR DIARY
or
INTELLIGENCE SUMMARY
(Erase heading not required.)

Army Form C. 2118

in before with arrangements that had already been made. A local attack took place but did not succeed to commence at 9.30 p.m. and of this we were not successful a second attack has been arranged to take place at 3.0 a.m. preceded by a bombardment which would commence at 1.0 a.m. and in any case the Officer Commanding the Black Watch Battalion in front trench was to be counseled regarding possible in reference with him ration, water & ammunition parties in the Communication trenches.

The posts needed an through the village of FESTUBERT and down to form on the supports trench where the Commanding Officers were interviewed. They were not encouraging. There was a good deal of rifle & machine gun fire going on and some shelling and they stated that they could get no information whatever as to the progress of operation in fire trench as wires

Army Form C. 2118

WAR DIARY
or
INTELLIGENCE SUMMARY
(Erase heading not required.)

Instructions regarding War Diaries and Intelligence Summaries are contained in F.S. Regs., Part II. and the Staff Manual respectively. Title Pages will be prepared in manuscript.

Place	Date	Hour	Summary of Events and Information	Remarks and references to Appendices
			were cut and no message by any? had reached them; the fatigue parties were at present many the communicating trenches and a good deal of ammunition had to be taken up to the fire trench before the second attack at 3.0 am ‑ could probably be necessary, and it appears that some support wd^d probably have been detailed in the early part of the night to go out & repair the broken wire and they had received working parties to bring in any wounded who might still be alive & endeavour to bring in near them. After consideration the decision was reluctantly come to that in all the circumstances the attempt to go further must be abandoned. The packs of the battalion which has been left at the nearer trenches before the attack were carried back to the village of FESTUBERT and stowed in a	

WAR DIARY
or
INTELLIGENCE SUMMARY

Army Form C. 2118

transport wagons which has been brought
the party set out on the return road
CORNET MALO which was reached about 4.30 am
on Friday morning. The men were very tired and were
not in a condition to bear much fatigue.

During the course of the day (Thursday 17th) intimation
has been received from No 4 Casualty Clearing Station
at LILLERS that 2nd Lieutenant W. R. WISHART
had died of his wounds

WAR DIARY
or
INTELLIGENCE SUMMARY
(Erase heading not required.)

Place	Date	Hour	Summary of Events and Information	Remarks and references to Appendices
	Friday 18th June		The Command of that remained of the Battalion then devolves upon Capt. A.G. GRAHAM, who while not of hospital still suffers from a sprained knee which renders walking difficult. It was decided that Captain J LUSK would perform the duties of Adjutant and Lt. & Quartermaster J. HAMILTON would carry out the duties of transport Officer as well as his own. The Company Commanders were the remaining available officers namely:— "A" Coy. Lieut. T.H. CAMPBELL "B" Coy. Lieut. F.J.C. WILSON "C" Coy. Lieut. D. RALSTON The senior of Lieut. J.C.E. HAY was applied to the Brigade who replied that there would be any.	

WAR DIARY
or
INTELLIGENCE SUMMARY
(Erase heading not required.)

Army Form C. 2118

Place	Date	Hour	Summary of Events and Information	Remarks and references to Appendices
	Saturday 19th June		In the morning Brigadier General C.L. HIBBERT Comdg. 151st Inf Bde came to Batln Headrs and as much of the action as was known was described to him in detail. He arranged to inspect the Battalion next day at an hour to be notified later. — Inspection of Battn by Brig General C.L. HIBBERT D.S.O. Comdg 151st Inf Bde at 11.20 am. He said he had been asked by General SIR HENRY RAWLINSON Comdg. IVth Army Corps to thank the Battalion for the splendid work they had done on the night of 15/16th June. Their Conduct deserved the highest praise, and he had no doubt that when rested and refitted the Regiment would be prepared to do the same	

WAR DIARY
or
INTELLIGENCE SUMMARY.
(Erase heading not required.)

Army Form C. 2118.

Hour, Date, Place	Summary of Events and Information	Remarks and references to Appendices
	again of Callipan. He deeply regretted the very heavy losses sustained, and although the attack had not been entirely successful the Br. had done what had been asked of them and their action had has an important influence upon the operations at other portions of the allies line. JL.	One man admitted to hospital today. JL.
Sunday 20th June.	Church Parade at 10.30 am Circumstances strangely different from last parade in same fields one week ago. Very many has gone. Service impressive in its simplicity & sincerity. The following Special Order was issued by Brigadier General Cundy, 154th Inf. Bde. JL.	

WAR DIARY
or
~~INTELLIGENCE SUMMARY.~~

(Erase heading not required.)

Army Form C. 2118.

Place	Hour, Date, Place	Summary of Events and Information	Remarks and references to Appendices
Place:— LE CORNET MALO (between MERVILLE and BETHUNE; & Several Kilos NW of FESTUBERT.)		Special Order by Brigadier General G. t. Hibbert D.S.O Commanding 154th Infantry Brigade. The Brigadier has received personal instructions from Lieut. General Sir H. Rawlinson commanding IVth Corps to convey to the Brigade his appreciation of the gallantry shown by all ranks in the attacks of the 15th and 16th instant under very trying circumstances. The Brigadier wishes to add on his own behalf his appreciation for the pluck and spirit evinced by all and while to deplore the heavy losses incurred congratulate the Brigade in the fine fighting qualities displayed (Signed) G.D Price Major Brigade Major 154th Infantry Brigade 18/6/15	

Army Form C. 2118.

WAR DIARY
or
INTELLIGENCE SUMMARY.
(Erase heading not required.)

Hour, Date, Place	Summary of Events and Information	Remarks and references to Appendices
Monday 21st June	Inspected by Major General Sir R. Bannatyne-Allason, C.B. Comdg. 51st (Highland) Division at 11 am. — together with 1/4th Royal Lancers to Regt. ("King's Own") Brig. Genl. Hibbert D.S.O. were also present. The inspecting officer thanked the Battalion for the splendid fighting qualities they had shown in the recent attack. The behaviour of the Regt. was in every way worthy of its highest traditions. The losses has been severe & no one regrets them more than he did, but we must "carry on". He has no doubt whatever that the Regt. if called upon again to show its mettle would surpass its own best record. JL.	JL. Sir been admitted to hospital today JL.

Army Form C. 2118.

WAR DIARY
or
INTELLIGENCE SUMMARY.
(Erase heading not required.)

Instructions regarding War Diaries and Intelligence Summaries are contained in F.S. Regs., Part II and the Staff Manual respectively. Title pages will be prepared in manuscript.

Hour, Date, Place	Summary of Events and Information	Remarks and references to Appendices
Tuesday 22nd June	Company work in vicinity of Billets. At 5 pm moved forward again to what the Divin described as an intermediate position at village of LA TOMB E WILLOT. Billets found very dirty & insanitary & reported so to Brigade. Sit was admitted throughout today.	
Wednesday 23rd June	Company work in vicinity of Billets in morning. Later in a never camp from Brigade calling for a working party of 200 men & "full proportion of Officers" to report at a certain form field by map reference not far behind trench line. Sufficient Equipment was collected & furnished this party	

(73989) W 4141—463. 400,000. 9/14. H.&J.Ltd. Forms/C. 2118/10.

WAR DIARY
or
INTELLIGENCE SUMMARY.
(Erase heading not required.)

Army Form C. 2118.

Hour, Date, Place	Summary of Events and Information	Remarks and references to Appendices
	which marched off at 5pm and Lieut Roberts, accompanied by Lieuts. Hay, Campbell & J.J.C. McIvor. The party returned at 4.30 am & reported having been at work upon a light railway & a Communication Trench. Sit. was admitted Satisfactory stop.	
Thursday 24th June	All men not out with working parts in previous night did physical exercises & drill in morning under senior NCOs of Companies. An order came that Brigade was to be prepared to march to a new area above Operation order Came later & it shewed that whole of 51st (Highland) Division was to march by night to ESTAIRES via LESTREM. This new zone the	

WAR DIARY
or
INTELLIGENCE SUMMARY
(Erase heading not required.)

Army Form C. 2118.

Hour, Date, Place	Summary of Events and Information	Remarks and references to Appendices
	Battalion the greatest satisfaction in nothing could be more pleasing than to get away from a district that had been for them the most unhappy association. The 6th Seo. Rifles took its place in the column by passing the costing point at 9 pm & reached its old billets in Sactm close to river LYS in ESTAIRES about midnight. Capt Graham & 4 NCOs has gone off in morning by motor bus to Headqrs of much respected 23rd Inf Bde to see trenches & improvements taken over by Battalion. I met the Battalion as it was marching into ESTAIRES. Jan was admits stopped today. JL.	

WAR DIARY or INTELLIGENCE SUMMARY.

Army Form C. 2118.

Hour, Date, Place	Summary of Events and Information	Remarks and references to Appendices
Friday 25th June	Morning spent in ESTAIRES standing by waiting for orders to move again. At 5 pm B" with its transport marched off to LAVENTIE less than three miles distant, which we reached in very heavy rain. Billeted in main street not far from the shell battered church. Two VICKERS MAXIM machine guns issued to 8" machine Gun Officer described them as very light & highly satisfactory. Four men admitted to hospital to-day.	

WAR DIARY
or
INTELLIGENCE SUMMARY.
(Erase heading not required.)

Army Form C. 2118.

Instructions regarding War Diaries and Intelligence Summaries are contained in F.S. Regs., Part II. and the Staff Manual respectively. Title pages will be prepared in manuscript.

Hour, Date, Place	Summary of Events and Information	Remarks and references to Appendices
Saturday 26th June	Physical exercises & Company drill in vicinity of Billets in morning. Bombers & Machine Gun Section practise in afternoon. Still no definite news about trench duty. One man admitted to hospital today. SL.	
Sunday 27th June	C.O. & Actg. Adjt. went to Headqrs 1/23rd Inf Bde to make arrangements for taking over a section of trenches that night. Brigade Major (Lysett) and BdE also present. Again pointed out shortage of Officers , when it was agreed to return Lieut Gray temporarily to Bn. In visiting the vicinity of LAVENTIE Church was again shelled & one of our men attending the bombing school at LAVENTIE was slightly wounded.	

(73989) W4141—463. 400,000. 9/14. H.&J.Ltd. Forms/C. 2118/10.

WAR DIARY or INTELLIGENCE SUMMARY

Army Form C. 2118.

Hour, Date, Place	Summary of Events and Information	Remarks and references to Appendices
At 10 pm	the Bn. has taken over from 2/Middlesex Regt. Section of "E" lines of trenches including three posts known as E3, E4, & Post 11, with a strength of 290 men & 5 officers (exclusive of C.O. & Actg. Adjt.) At midnight a good deal of firing was being done by other Regiment on our right. The right hand Surrey Patrol reported enemy working party on our front, but otherwise situation quiet. Two motor machine guns with their teams under their own officer advice in this section of the trenches were placed near the Battalion Hqrs. This made the guns on the front held by Battalion	Three men admitted to hospital today.

Army Form C. 2118.

WAR DIARY
or
INTELLIGENCE SUMMARY.
(Erase heading not required.)

Instructions regarding War Diaries and Intelligence Summaries are contained in F.S. Regs., Part II and the Staff Manual respectively. Title pages will be prepared in manuscript.

Hour, Date, Place	Summary of Events and Information	Remarks and references to Appendices
Monday 28th June	Day passed uneventfully. Brigadier General Hibbert visited trenches in afternoon & made suggestions to various works behind parapet. Night of 28/29th was without incident. Work was carried out on parapet & communication trenches & wire in front of parapet was repaired. One man admitted Hospital. JL	

WAR DIARY or INTELLIGENCE SUMMARY.

Army Form C. 2118.

Hour, Date, Place	Summary of Events and Information	Remarks and references to Appendices
Tuesday 29th June	Day passed quietly. Bde Major visited French Headquarters in evening & explained details of certain works which were to be carried out. High of 29/30th bom- bardment save for the blowing up of one of our mines under German trench at about 1000 yards to left of our section. It was followed by our artillery fire from both sides, but of short duration. The Germans done by the mine could not be clearly seen. Two men admitted to hospital today. J.L.	

WAR DIARY
or
INTELLIGENCE SUMMARY.
(Erase heading not required.)

Army Form C. 2118.

Hour, Date, Place	Summary of Events and Information	Remarks and references to Appendices
Wednesday 30th June	Very little firing from either side until 2 pm when Enemy sent about 8 or 10 shells over French Headqrs. No damage was done. Night of 30/1 passed quiet. Some signalling with lamps was observed from Enemy's line & duly reported to Bryde. Work was done on repairs to parapet etc. JL.	Repeated in "June Diary"
Thursday 1st July	Trenches were inspected at 9 am by Divisional General accompanied by Brigadier General. A carrier pigeon was observed about 6.70pm flying across trenches from enemy lines towards our lines & was duly reported to Brigade. Night of 1/2 July passed quietly. Repairs were carried out to parapet & dugouts. One man admitted to hospital. JL.	

51st Div.

~~Confidential~~

War Diary
of
1/6th Scottish Rifles

From 1st July 1915 to 31st July 1915

Vol LI

Army Form C. 2118

WAR DIARY
or
INTELLIGENCE SUMMARY
(Erase heading not required.)

Instructions regarding War Diaries and Intelligence Summaries are contained in F. S. Regs., Part II. and the Staff Manual respectively. Title Pages will be prepared in manuscript.

Place	Date	Hour	Summary of Events and Information	Remarks and references to Appendices
	Thursday 1st July		Trenches were inspected by Divisional General accompanied by Brigadier General at 9. a.m. A carrier pigeon was observed about 6.30 pm flying across trenches from enemy's lines towards our lines. was duly reported to Brigade. Night 1/2. July parties busily Repairs were carried out on parapets & dugouts. One man admitted to hospital today.	

WAR DIARY
or
INTELLIGENCE SUMMARY.
(Erase heading not required.)

Army Form C. 2118.

Hour, Date, Place	Summary of Events and Information	Remarks and references to Appendices
Sunday 2nd July	Brigadier General Canny, 153rd Brigade went round trenches with Brigadier General Canny 153rd Bde in connection with the taking over of the section by the latter Brigade on Saturday night 3/4 July. In afternoon a party of officers of 7th Black Watch went round our section & made arrangements about taking over on Saturday night. Carrier pigeons again reported flying over trenches towards our lines. About 2.30 a.m. an enemy aeroplane dropped a bomb on the left of the Battalion. The Battalion was standing to arms when the firing began & it was thought that this	

WAR DIARY
or
INTELLIGENCE SUMMARY.
(Erase heading not required.)

Army Form C. 2118.

Hour, Date, Place	Summary of Events and Information	Remarks and references to Appendices
	might be the prelude of an enemy attack. Several shells dropped behind the Battalion Section of the fire trench and just missed a listening post garrisoned by a few of our men. The fire personnel did adm. however, and our men have not yet recovered from the strain of their recent experiences of 15/16th June. One man admitted to hospital.	
Saturday 3rd July	Machine Gun Officer of 7th Black Watch came in afternoon to arrange about taking over. His two guns arrived at 7 pm & relief of our machine gun section was complete at 8.15 pm. The relieving Battalion arrived at French Head Sqrs. at 9 pm & relief was reported	A draft of 8 officers arrived from home names as below:- Capt. T Watt Lieut J. Main 2/Lieut R. Spiers 2/Lieut J.A. Jackson " E.B. Bayly " Geo Denholm " A.C. Bay G.

WAR DIARY
or
INTELLIGENCE SUMMARY.
(Erase heading not required.)

Army Form C. 2118.

Hour, Date, Place	Summary of Events and Information	Remarks and references to Appendices
	So complete at 10.25 pm. The relieving Battalion had the relief a longer process than need have been by insisting on the issue of sandbags to them in so they went to our trenches. The Battalion marched by Companies to LE DRUMEZ vis LAVENTIE trenches - St - huts at about 11.30 pm.	
Sunday 4th July	Church Parade at 12.30 pm in Transport field. Minor came from Pte Hal. 1544 St. Pte was inspected in manor afternoon by Commander of Indian Corps. He went on Sund 5th of River LYS from Opposite ESTAIRES Church. Six officers attended lecture on bombing at LAVENTIE at 5.20 pm.	One man wounded in trenches on 5 day.

WAR DIARY
or
INTELLIGENCE SUMMARY.
(Erase heading not required.)

Army Form C. 2118.

Hour, Date, Place	Summary of Events and Information	Remarks and references to Appendices
Monday 5th July	"A" & "B" Companies paraded at LA GORGUE Baths at 7am & 8am respectively. Men parade with clean clothing. This much appreciated by men as they had not had since last luxury of this kind been rather long. At 2.30 pm Brigade was drawn up ready for inspection by Lieut. General Sir James Willcocks Comdg. Indian Corps. to which the 51st (Joyles?) Division we belong. Each Battalion was inspected in turn, and thereafter all the dismount officers paraded in front of the Brigade & were congratulated upon their work at FESTUBERT during the recent fighting there.	

WAR DIARY
or
INTELLIGENCE SUMMARY.
(Erase heading not required.)

Army Form C. 2118.

Hour, Date, Place	Summary of Events and Information	Remarks and references to Appendices
	Sir James Wilcocks then shook hands with every officer & warrant officer on parade and enquired as to their length of service etc. The Brigade marched past in Column of route. A working party was called for & report was tendered at 9.15 pm. The numbers called for could not be furnished by the Battalion. This was reported to Brigade + all available men to the number of 230 were sent under Command of 2/Lieut R. Spiers — one of the officers recently joined from Reserve Battn. Party returned safely about 3.30 am on 6/7/15.	

WAR DIARY
or
INTELLIGENCE SUMMARY.
(Erase heading not required.)

Army Form C. 2118.

Hour, Date, Place	Summary of Events and Information	Remarks and references to Appendices
Tuesday 6th July	Working party of 50 again called for. Paraded at 3 am 7/7/15 new trenches. Five Officers attended lecture on Bombing at LAVENTIE at 5.20 pm. Two men admitted to hospital today.	
Wednesday 7th July	Company Drill + Physical Exercises carried out in morning. Working party of 200 men collected to work on Light Railway being constructed near trenches. They returned about 3 am. Six men admitted to hospital today.	

WAR DIARY
or
INTELLIGENCE SUMMARY.
(Erase heading not required.)

Army Form C. 2118.

Hour, Date, Place	Summary of Events and Information	Remarks and references to Appendices

Thursday 8th July

No divisional parade. Another working party of 150 men called for to report to 1/1 N Midland Coy RE at 9.15 pm and a further one of 40 men at 2 am. These working parties make it impossible to continue the proper training of the men, as the Coy have to find the Divisional in addition to the whole self & my trying Co. & M. orders to attend Brigade Head Qrs mid-day to taking over a section of trenches on Friday night.

Two men admitted to hospital today.

WAR DIARY
or
INTELLIGENCE SUMMARY.

(Erase heading not required.)

Army Form C. 2118.

Hour, Date, Place	Summary of Events and Information	Remarks and references to Appendices
Friday 9th July	Marched off at 7.30pm to trenches. Section allotted to us was a section of F line also Posts F2 and F3. This portion of the fire trench includes the "Salient" which the Battalion held in the last. In this district was 8th Division. The relief was complete at 10.15pm, the Battalion relieved being 7th Beaconwatch of 152nd Bde. High found swing Justin Shutt was admitted to hospital today. M	

WAR DIARY
or
INTELLIGENCE SUMMARY.
(Erase heading not required.)

Army Form C. 2118.

Hour, Date, Place	Summary of Events and Information	Remarks and references to Appendices
Saturday 10th July	Day passed without incident. At night work was done on proper & Sirari was cut between our lines & those of the enemy. This from has been allowed to grow too long & gives too much cover to any one approaching our lines. night piquets supplied.	
Sunday 11th July	Day quiet. During night there was a good deal of rifle fire on our right but nothing noteworthy occurred on our immediate front. Work was continued on grass cut on wire & parapet. Three men admitted to hospital today.	

WAR DIARY
or
INTELLIGENCE SUMMARY
(Erase heading not required.)

Army Form C. 2118.

Hour, Date, Place	Summary of Events and Information	Remarks and references to Appendices
Monday 12th July	Enemy active with trench mortars during day, wounding 2 men one of whom is Sweeney, hurt & heavy repeated tremor. During the day one of our snipers was hit by rifle bullet while using rifle with telescopic sights. In the evening L/Cpl McGee in charge of listening post was struck in head by rifle bullet while on road behind lines. The wound is severe. Work continued during night on general cutting and repairs & parapet shrine. Saps were also started from the front parapet advances to act as listening posts. Four men enlisted in Khedival today	

Army Form C. 2118.

WAR DIARY
or
INTELLIGENCE SUMMARY.
(Erase heading not required.)

Instructions regarding War Diaries and Intelligence Summaries are contained in F.S. Regs., Part II. and the Staff Manual respectively. Title pages will be prepared in manuscript.

Hour, Date, Place	Summary of Events and Information	Remarks and references to Appendices
Sunday 13th July	Day passed quietly. In evening a draft of two officers from home arrived. These names are Major Kirsop, G.S. Laurie 2/Lieut. R.G.M. London. Work was continued during night, repairing wire, putting out cheveaux de frise, cutting long grass & continuing the making of listening posts. The night passed without incident of importance. Two men admitted to hospital.	
Wednesday 14th July	During the greater part of the day a heavy bombardment had been going on on our right but it seemed the some distance off. Our own front has quiet. Night was very dark & wet & little work could be undertaken. One man admitted to hospital	

WAR DIARY
or
INTELLIGENCE SUMMARY.

Army Form C. 2118.

Hour, Date, Place	Summary of Events and Information	Remarks and references to Appendices
Thursday 15th July	Day passed quietly. Little firing on either side. Battn was relieved in trenches by 1/14 Royal Lancers to Right and by 2/5th Lancashire Fusiliers to left. Reliefs of the posts taken over by the Somer Regt. were complete by 10.25pm but that of the Lancs was not completed until 11.30pm. The delay was entirely due to want of sufficient carrying arrangements in taking over & due to movement of our premises in support of this Battn relieving us. The Battn withdrew to Posts 17 & 18 near RUE BACQUEROT & to huts in the above road and is now in Brigade Reserve. Two Divisions Brickfield.	

WAR DIARY or INTELLIGENCE SUMMARY

Hour, Date, Place	Summary of Events and Information	Remarks and references to Appendices
Friday 16th July	Working parts furnished for work on support trench. Strength 50 men. Rest seems impossible. Great importance seems to be attached to these line works at present & all available men are called for. Major J. Livingstone London RAMC(T) took leave of the Battalion this evening & take up duties at a hospital in HAVRE. He will be much missed by the Battalion to his work under the most trying circumstances has been beyond all praise. He is succeeded by Lieut T.H. Morsat RAMC(T) who has come from hospital work at Havre	

WAR DIARY or INTELLIGENCE SUMMARY

Army Form C. 2118.

Hour, Date, Place	Summary of Events and Information	Remarks and references to Appendices
Saturday 17th July	Work has been commenced upon the two Pols held by Battalion. These are being converted from a disconnected series of dugouts into a proper fortified post, of which the chief defensive work is a well built trench around a water supply. In the centre a number of dugouts with strong shell proof roofs. Lieut. D. RALSTON & J.C.E. HAY left for a week's leave in Scotland. Church parade for all available men at 9 p.m.	
Sunday 18th July	12 noon. Working parts of S.O. men have furnished as born at M. Heasp. No casualties. One admitted to Hospital.	

WAR DIARY
or
INTELLIGENCE SUMMARY.
(Erase heading not required.)

Army Form C. 2118.

Hour, Date, Place	Summary of Events and Information	Remarks and references to Appendices
Sunday 18th July	The Assistant Director of Medical Services 51st (Highland) Division has to-day congratulated the Battalion upon the general cleanliness of the Section of the trenches recently occupied by it. He considers that the high standard attained by the Battalion in this matter reflects the greatest credit upon all concerned, and made a special visit to Batt. Headqrs in person to inform the Commanding Officer on the subject. The percentage figure of cleanliness assigned to the Battalion as the result of an inspection carried out at a time unknown to it was 98%.	

WAR DIARY
or
INTELLIGENCE SUMMARY.
(Erase heading not required.)

Army Form C. 2118.

Hour, Date, Place	Summary of Events and Information	Remarks and references to Appendices
Monday 19th July	Work continued on Posts. R.E. stores here easily obtained for this - One adminin Khakine.	
Tuesday 20th July.	Work again continued. They were no opportunity for drill & the Battn. wants to meet the whole of it - Work posts for support trench again called for by Brigade. At 9 p.m. Brigade sent telephone message :- "Your Battalion will stand to arms at once." The posts were at once manned as directed in Defence Scheme remainder of Battalion stand by in Alarm Posts	

WAR DIARY
or
INTELLIGENCE SUMMARY.
(Erase heading not required.)

Army Form C. 2118.

Hour, Date, Place	Summary of Events and Information	Remarks and references to Appendices
	At 9.30 pm heavy fire Brigade came to "Stand down". Condition again normal. It is understood that alarm was due to the active imagination of one inexperienced Battalion in front line who, who made it known to all concerned that enemy were attacking in large numbers. It was a matter for some congratulation to the rest of us that the enemy were at that time unaware of what was expected of them. Working parts of 50 again furnished for work on support trench. No casualties. On admin to Hinghitove.	

WAR DIARY
or
INTELLIGENCE SUMMARY.
(Erase heading not required.)

Army Form C. 2118.

Hour, Date, Place	Summary of Events and Information	Remarks and references to Appendices
Wednesday 21st July	Work continued in Posts. Bursts of rapid machine gun & rifle fire heard from time to time in trenches.	
Thursday 22nd July	Work still continued. a Pte. Battalion advised that they request to relieve in Posts by 1st Middlesex Regt. 19th Inf. Bde. afternoon & evening & hoped to go back for a few days training. About 2½ miles N.W. of NEUF BERQUIN to entrain Journey to join another Corps was moved South to join another Corps & started that afternoon in finding billets for Battn. in this new area. Mitchell admins to hospital.	

WAR DIARY
or
INTELLIGENCE SUMMARY.

(Erase heading not required.)

Army Form C. 2118.

Hour, Date, Place	Summary of Events and Information	Remarks and references to Appendices
Friday 23rd July.	Move still continued. Picks heels by 5pm Bath. were taken over about 6pm by 1/5th Middlesex Regt. and at 10.30 pm remainder of Middlesex Regt. arrived at billets & time believed the Bn. to move to Rr. Billet in the new area of NEUF BERQUIN were reached at about 1.0 am. The night been cool and a good hour made marching easy.	
Saturday 24th July	Definite orders were received from the 15th Inf. Bde. as to the Entrainment of the Battalion, including Railway Time Table, & station of detrainment. One admission to hospital	

Army Form C. 2118.

WAR DIARY
or
INTELLIGENCE SUMMARY.
(Erase heading not required.)

Instructions regarding War Diaries and Intelligence Summaries are contained in F.S. Regs., Part II and the Staff Manual respectively. Title pages will be prepared in manuscript.

Hour, Date, Place	Summary of Events and Information	Remarks and references to Appendices
Sunday 25th July	Church Parade at 10.30 a.m. This Parade was the strongest that the Battn. has held for some time as the Bombers, Trench Mortar Teams, and mining Section has all been returned to the Bn. In the period of the move. Riding School was held in afternoon for benefit of Younger Officers who had just joined. Captains RALSTON & HAY returned from leave - having been promoted to rank of Temp. Captain. One admission to hospital.	
Monday 26th July	Adt. Asst. & Adt. Transport Officer visited LA GORGUE Station in morning to inspect facilities for entraining, whilst Companies carried out programme of work, consisting	

WAR DIARY
or
INTELLIGENCE SUMMARY.
(Erase heading not required.)

Army Form C. 2118.

Hour, Date, Place	Summary of Events and Information	Remarks and references to Appendices
Tuesday 27th July	Close order drill, musketry and handling of arms. Recruit school again held in afternoon & one admission attached. In morning Companies carried out Company drill etc. in fields near their Billets. At 11pm the whole of the Transport Section accompanied by extra D Company (to act as loading party) marched off from Pillis' to LA GORGUE Station & entrained for new area. The loading facilities being quite satisfactory and within 1½ hours the time of arrival at station every horse vehicle on board in railway trucks. The entraining of the animals was	

WAR DIARY
or
INTELLIGENCE SUMMARY.
(Erase heading not required.)

Army Form C. 2118.

Instructions regarding War Diaries and Intelligence Summaries are contained in F. S. Regs., Part II. and the Staff Manual respectively. Title pages will be prepared in manuscript.

Hour, Date, Place	Summary of Events and Information	Remarks and references to Appendices
	accomplished with very little difficulty. Occasionally a mule declined to go up the inclined gangway to the railway truck at the first time of asking, but the prejudice was overcome by a little be-hind pressure on the broader of the vehicle. did not present much difficulty as there were plenty of men furnished to handle them easily. (Guard) The entraining strength of the Battn was 15 Officers, one hundred Officer attached, one Interpreter attached, and 470 other ranks; 72 animals and 23 vehicles. Nine covered trucks accommodated the 72 animals and 18 covered trucks the 470 other ranks. (being aware of 26 per truck) While the Officers had one passenger coach.	

WAR DIARY
or
INTELLIGENCE SUMMARY.
(Erase heading not required.)

Army Form C. 2118.

Hour, Date, Place	Summary of Events and Information	Remarks and references to Appendices
Wednesday 28th July	The Railway Time Table was as follows:— LA GORGUE — Dep. 4.03 CALAIS — Arr. 7.53 " — Dep. 9.01 ABBEVILLE — Arr. 13.27 " — Dep. 14.37 AMIENS — Arr. 16.10 CORBIE — Arr. 17.03 The journey was of considerable interest as the country was at its best, and a great portion had not been seen for months. The permanent side of the journey was a change of view & surroundings. Very satisfactory arrangements had been made at the two halts at CALAIS and ABBEVILLE for the provision of refreshments for the men, &	

WAR DIARY
or
INTELLIGENCE SUMMARY
(Erase heading not required.)

Army Form C. 2118

Place	Date	Hour	Summary of Events and Information	Remarks and references to Appendices
			The outskirts of CALAIS & BOULOGNE were passed with mingled feelings as to when they might be seen again under happier circumstances. The light of the sea was most refreshing. Captain Paton left the train at BOULOGNE for 8 days leave and CORBIE was reached at 5.0 pm. Detraining was quickly carried out first by the Battalion & next by the transport section assisted again by "D" Company. The Regiment was complicated by the R.T.O. upon the admirable supervision with which the detraining had been carried out. There followed a march of about 5 miles through beautiful country — hilly, well wooded & with fields carried with ripe crops. Billets were assigned for the Battn. in the village of RIBEMONT with B. Headqrs in an old French Chateau much neglected but still most attractive. This was reached about 8 pm. (Nd admin in hospital)	

Place	Date	Hour	Summary of Events and Information	Remarks and references to Appendices
	Thursday 29th July		Companies bathed in river in early part of afternoon. Acting ADC went to Bde. Head qrs to arrange to attend a lecture on "D' Infantin". It was spoken of as taking over of a portion of trench line from the 22nd Regiment. It was there arranged that the 1/8 Liverpool Regt. would hold the right sector of the Brigade's frontage & the 2/5th Lancashire Fusiliers wd hold the left sector. The Brigade front extended to about 3400 yards but it was explained that the front was not constituted [or being manned] continuously owing to it irregular outline. Many posts were easily commanded by other posts and there would be 8 machine guns to the Brigade's front line. Two Companies were to be in support of the right sector and the other two Coys in support of the left sector. The Batt.ns were thus sub divided, each half being stationed about 500 yds behind firing line and separated from the other half by a distance of about 1100 yds. One division in Trophone	

Place	Date	Hour	Summary of Events and Information	Remarks and references to Appendices
	Friday 30th July		At 4 pm the 154th Inf. Bde. was inspected by General Sir C.C. Monro, K.C.B., Commanding IIIrd Army. He was accompanied by Commander of Xth Corps & by Commander of 51st (Highland) Division. He arrived at Parade Ground by Motor Car and carried out his inspection on foot, shaking hands with each Company Officer. The G.O.C. shot Rifles was the last to which is diminished size frequently to the General Officer Conding. Brigade. "These fellows forget well, did they not". Major General Lyndon-Bell who accompanied the Inspecting Officer called his attention to Sergt. R. Downie in the ranks as having been awarded the D.C.M. whereupon he shook hands with Sergt Downie & complimented him on his Service.	

Place	Date	Hour	Summary of Events and Information	Remarks and references to Appendices
			At 10.30 pm the Battn. together with its Transport set out from RIBEMONT to BOUZINCOURT about 6 miles distant. The moon was clear and the road was hilly, and Billets were reached about 1 am. Fine admiring the hind.	
	Saturday 31st July		The Act. Adj. left BOUZINCOURT at 7 am and reported with his other Commanding Officers at a Chateau in AVELUY at 8am, which was the Headqrs of 22nd Regiment D'Infanterie. The road led through the village of ALBERT which has received a great deal of attention from German Artillery. It is on the top of the tower of the large Church in the village that we see what has been so often illustrated in the press of Great Britain, namely the gilt figure of the Virgin Mary with the Child in her arms so completely bent	

WAR DIARY
or
INTELLIGENCE SUMMARY
(Erase heading not required.)

Army Form C. 2118

Place	Date	Hour	Summary of Events and Information	Remarks and references to Appendices
			Over at the pedestal that it overhangs the shelf below. Only the twisted metal framework of the base of the statue holds it in position and prevents it from falling to the ground. At the Chateau guides were furnished by the French Army to take Commanding Officers over section of trenches allotted to Battalions. The trenches previous to the very well constructed and the wire in front specially abundant and strong. At frequent intervals along the trench line there are excavated very deep shelters against Artillery bombardment approached by a long flight of steps and received founded with two entrances. These might hold 50 or 60 men at a time. The front line is well provided with trenches dug out towards the enemy lines as listening posts and posts for artillery observation, these trenches are always commanded by a loophole in the front parapet	

WAR DIARY
or
INTELLIGENCE SUMMARY
(Erase heading not required.)

Army Form C. 2118

Place	Date	Hour	Summary of Events and Information	Remarks and references to Appendices
			The French have a system of burying their Trenches after officers who have been killed in action near the place concerned. They also make up of outstanding names connected with the war & name their communication trenches & there are all shown on their trench maps. No cooking was permitted in the front line trenches. It was all done about 1000 yards back under shelter and carried up to the men in the front line. The French seemed to dislike the presence of smoke as being liable to draw the enemy's fire and seemed unable to appreciate the British argument that as the presence of our troops was always well known to the enemy, columns of smoke (behind the trench line gave nothing away that was not already known. The French system knew probably has the advantage in that it is easier to keep trenches clean, and fewer flies congregate where there is less refuse and no cooking	

WAR DIARY or INTELLIGENCE SUMMARY

The Battalion marched off to trenches at 7.40 p.m. from BOUZINCOURT via ALBERT and AVELUY a distance of about 5 or 6 miles, accompanied by French guides. A & B Companies occupied a position known as POSTE DONNET while C & D Companies occupied a similar position known as POSTE LES DOS. Battn Headqrs were at the latter Post. The former Post consisted of a long trench well furnished with shelters that appeared to be bullet proof & access to the front line trench was obtained by several communication trenches dug in ground that consisted chiefly of white chalk. This chalk had been thrown up alongside the trench & for a period I was certain exceedingly conspicuous. The officers quarters at this post were of the most palatial description & so close to the firing line

WAR DIARY
or
INTELLIGENCE SUMMARY
(Erase heading not required.)

Army Form C. 2118

Place	Date	Hour	Summary of Events and Information	Remarks and references to Appendices
			The Batto Post was in a wood the edge of which touched the firing line. The shelters had been deeply dug and strongly built & the French Army had bestowed so much of their natural artistic ingenuity upon the place that it resembled nothing so much as some rustic tea garden in the midst of a City Park. Table chairs timber balconies pavements hand rails and arbours seemed to take one far from thoughts of war till bought back to reality by the strength of a shell through the trees. It was remarkable to notice how very much louder the explosion of a shell or the crack of a rifle sounded in this wood than it did on the plains of FLANDERS. There were trenches facing north & facing south which would be manned by the Battalion in case the front line Battalion should be attacked from either direction. Two admissions to hospital.	

51st T.M.

Confidential

War Diary
of
1/6th Scottish Rifles

From 1st August 1915. To 31st August 1915.

Vol III

WAR DIARY or INTELLIGENCE SUMMARY

Army Form C. 2118

Place	Date	Hour	Summary of Events and Information	Remarks and references to Appendices
	Sunday 1st August		The night passed quietly. The day follows by a quiet day, during which the men settled down to their new surroundings. Cooking & washing facilities presented a difficult problem under the restrictions imposed. The policy of the Trench Army in the matter of improving the defensive system of the position was continued by us & accordingly work was carried on by day and by night upon trenches & the approaches to them & north of the posts occupied. There was little firing on either side. A French officer remained with Headqrs during each Company's tour to re-hearse after relief the working parties.	4 admins taught on 3 Whitehead cases. 3 of these were rec'd as stretcher wounds received by Reserve M.G. team in AVELUY.
	Monday 2nd August		Night passed uneventfully even for the working parties. The day also passed without incident.	

WAR DIARY
or
INTELLIGENCE SUMMARY

Army Form C. 2118

Place	Date	Hour	Summary of Events and Information	Remarks and references to Appendices
	Tuesday 3rd Aug.		Work was continued upon the defences, during night, and day parties without incident. Three men of Bn. suffering from one admission to hospital. Various forms of lameness were attached today to "Divisional Sabray's Company".	
	Wednesday 4 Aug.		Work again continued. About 1pm some shrapnel came over its wood which we had a head, not serious. 4 admissions to hospital, one of which was a case of slight shrapnel wound.	
	Thursday 5 Aug.		Work continued, including repairs to road through wood. About 9-10 pm some shelling of road took place, but without damage. Intimation received from Brigade that Capt. F.J.C. WILSON had been accepted for permanent employment with Royal Regt. of Corps as from 2nd August. (Two admissions to hospital)	

WAR DIARY or INTELLIGENCE SUMMARY

Place	Date	Hour	Summary of Events and Information	Remarks and references to Appendices
	Friday 6th Aug		Work still continued; occasional shells are sent into the road & several to right and to each day toward AVELUY and ALBERT. Orders are received that the Battn will have its front line of trenches on night of 7/8th Aug, the 1/4 Kings our Royal Lancaster Regt in its right and the 1/4 Loyal North Lancashire Regt on its left, and in the purpose of this tour of trench duty the orders add that the 6th Co. Rifles will be under the Command of the O.C. 1/4 Loyal North Lanc Regt. For tactical operations but will remain under its own Comdt. Officer for administration and discipline. It is difficult to find a reason for this awkward change in Command other than the satisfactory one that the 154th Inf. Bde may doubtless consider it a convenience to treat the line of its frontier as being held by two Battalions instead of by three. Coy Commanders & Act. Adjt went round front line to be occupied. One admin in hospital.	

WAR DIARY
or
INTELLIGENCE SUMMARY

Army Form C. 2118

Place	Date	Hour	Summary of Events and Information	Remarks and references to Appendices
	Saturday 7th Aug.		By arrangement with the A.D.M.S. 51st (H.) Div'n Lieut T.H. Morat R.A.M.C.(T) attached to 6th Sea: Rifles since 16th July transferred to 5th Seaforth Highlanders, a regiment with whose recruiting locality Lt. Morat has been long connected. His place in hadn't Group of 6th Sea: Rifles was filled by the appointment of Lieut. W.W. Turner, R.A.M.C.(T). Capt. A.G. Graham returned from leave, having been promoted temp. Major. The taking over of trenches was accomplished without any difficulty in the late afternoon. 1/th 53rd Bde. A platoon of one of the Essex Regts of the 18th Division they "has Army" was attached to each Company in the front line for instructional purposes. There was ample room for these additional troops without overcrowding the line. Two advancing troops Telegrafs.	

Army Form C. 2118

WAR DIARY
or
INTELLIGENCE SUMMARY
(Erase heading not required.)

Instructions regarding War Diaries and Intelligence Summaries are contained in F.S. Regs., Part II. and the Staff Manual respectively. Title Pages will be prepared in manuscript.

Place	Date	Hour	Summary of Events and Information	Remarks and references to Appendices
	Sunday 8th Aug.		It was discovered a takeing on trenches that thy has been left in an exhaustedly wearing condition by preceding regiment & matters were brought to the notice of the Brigade supported by medical Officers Report. The 6th & 7th Jos. Rifles at once took steps to treat this condition of affairs. Enemy machine gun fire swept the woods in evening & a desultory firing was kept up during the greater part of the night. One man was slightly hit by shrapnel in front of trench. One continuous to hospital.	
	Monday 9th August		Day passed without incident. Save occasional shelling of the wood. Desultory fire from rifles & machine guns kept up during greater part of night. Torrents of rain fell during night, accompanied by thunder & lightning. Shell ammunition to hospital – two of them having been slightly wounded by shrapnel.	

1875 Wt. W593/826 1,000,000 4/15 J.B.C. & A. A.D/S.S./Forms/C. 2118.

WAR DIARY
or
INTELLIGENCE SUMMARY
(Erase heading not required.)

Army Form C. 2118

Place	Date	Hour	Summary of Events and Information	Remarks and references to Appendices
	Tuesday 10th August		Trenches in exceptionally muddy state after rain of previous night. Fortunately there was sunshine which helped greatly to dry the men's clothing etc. The men were again treated to machine gun fire after dark. One admission to hospital.	
	Wednesday 11th Aug.		Day passed without incident. Night again broken by machine gun fire & a goodly dose of shells in the rear.	
	Thursday 12th Aug.		About 2 am a man named Pte J. Ritchie was killed by shell whilst out in front in a listening post. He was buried near AUTHUILLE amid torrents of rain in the afternoon. Three admissions to hospital.	

WAR DIARY
or
INTELLIGENCE SUMMARY
(Erase heading not required.)

Army Form C. 2118

Place	Date	Hour	Summary of Events and Information	Remarks and references to Appendices
	Friday 13th Aug.		night was quiet & the usual but trenches received special had after heavy rain. It was decided that Letter A. Coy would be the one left behind at POSTE LEIDOS a relief. Three admissions to hospital. Lieut. T.H. CAMPBELL left for 2 weeks leave in Scotland.	
	Saturday 14 Aug.		It was arranged that Battalion was to be relieved at 4 pm & moved with drawn to brigade Reserve in valley of AVELUY, later the Brigade orders no movements to take place till after dark. Accordingly the last Company was not relieved in trenches till about 10 pm & hill 6 was reached about 11 pm. Accommodation pretty Good, but duties so numerous that men have not much opportunity of real rest. Iron Garrison Posts (24 hours) have to be furnished and working parties found from the remainder of the Battn. two one Company.	

WAR DIARY or INTELLIGENCE SUMMARY

Army Form C. 2118

(Erase heading not required.)

Place	Date	Hour	Summary of Events and Information	Remarks and references to Appendices
	Sunday 15th April		Whilst one Company is on duty in the firing line the Company not in the firing line in the administrative trenches. Divine Service was held at 11.30 am for the only available Company namely "C" Coy. Work was commenced on the Construction of a series of shelters on side of hill intended eventually for use as a Battalion Canteen.	
	Monday 16 April		Work continues on shelters but considered unsafe until timber is available to support roofs. Men consequently withdrawn from this & transferred to the clearing of a track through new communication trenches	

WAR DIARY
or
INTELLIGENCE SUMMARY

Army Form C. 2118

Place	Date	Hour	Summary of Events and Information	Remarks and references to Appendices
			with the intention of digging a communication trench through wood for use during winter. 5 admissions to hospital.	
	Tuesday 17th Aug		Enemy sent a few shells into village about 8.45 am but no damage was done. In evening Letts "B" Coy relieved Letts "A" Coy in POSTES LEODOS, "A" Coy taking over hut ("hilts") vacated by "B" Coy. Work continued on trench in wood. Two NCOs and 15 men across the work underground are attached to 179th (Siege) Tunnelling Company, R.E. for "sapping" work. It is intended that these men be transferred to R.E. permanently. 5 admissions to hospital.	

Army Form C. 2118

WAR DIARY
or
INTELLIGENCE SUMMARY
(Erase heading not required.)

Instructions regarding War Diaries and Intelligence Summaries are contained in F.S. Regs., Part II. and the Staff Manual respectively. Title Pages will be prepared in manuscript.

Place	Date	Hour	Summary of Events and Information	Remarks and references to Appendices
	Wednesday 18th Aug		Work continued. Trench digging & wood clearing. At 5pm letter "B" Coy to be withdrawn from POSTE LESDOS to make room for a company of Newarmy sent to do duty in front line. Two admissions to hospital.	
	Thursday 19th Aug.		Work in wood continued. At 2pm "B" Coy returns to POSTE LESDOS. Two admissions to hospital.	
	Friday 20th Aug.		Work continued. Lieut B. Coy again withdrawn. Same reason. Brigade called for a return of Officers NCOs & men accustomed to woodcutting and forestry work. One admission to hospital.	

1875 Wt. W593/826 1,000,000 4/15 J.B.C. & A. A.D.S.S./Forms/C. 2118.

Army Form C. 2118

WAR DIARY
or
INTELLIGENCE SUMMARY
(Erase heading not required.)

Instructions regarding War Diaries and Intelligence Summaries are contained in F. S. Regs., Part II. and the Staff Manual respectively. Title Pages will be prepared in manuscript.

Place	Date	Hour	Summary of Events and Information	Remarks and references to Appendices
	Saturday 21st Aug.		Work continued - Later "B" Coy returned to POSTE LESDOS at 2 pm. Adjutant went to village of SENLIS in morning preceded by Billeting Party to take over billets from 1st Bn L'pool Regt. Divisional Reserve, returning to AVELUY. At about 9.30 pm the Battalion was relieved in Brigade Reserve & our companies marched off independently to SENLIS. Division al Reserve Billets were reached about 11.30 pm which we found only moderately clean. 5 men were sent the attached to Divisional MacCulloch Coy. Church Parade was held in a farm yard at one	One man admitted to hospital today. Capt. T.H. CAMPBELL returned from leave, having been promoted temp. Capt.
	Sunday 22nd Aug.		of the Company Billets at 11.30 am. Two working parties of 150 each were called for daily for work on intermediate line defences near BOUZINCOURT. It was pointed out that the Battn could not furnish	

Army Form C. 2118

WAR DIARY
or
INTELLIGENCE SUMMARY
(Erase heading not required.)

Place	Date	Hour	Summary of Events and Information	Remarks and references to Appendices
	Monday 23rd May		Two patrols of greater strength than before, viz. 120 each, left for duty village road guards & village scavenging Squad.	
			Iron working party marched off at 7.45 am after early breakfast & returned at 1.45 pm. Second party left billets at 12.45 pm & returned about 6 pm. In evening orders came from Division that the Battalion would move on Tuesday afternoon to villages of MARTINSART where it would remain in Divisional Reserve. The officer for employ was ordered to reconnoitre routes from MARTINSART & AUTHUILLE + Selger Post for use in Emergency.	3 admissions to hospital.
	Tuesday 24 May		Billeting Party under Capt J.C.E. Hay went to MARTINSART to prepare for arrival of Battalion. Battalion arrived about 5.30 pm and occupied billets vacated by Regiment Lancers. The subject of cleanliness & sanitation of billets had (evident) not received much attention from the latter.	15 men admitted to hospital today.

1875 Wt. W593/826 1,000,000 4/15 J.B.C. & A. A.D.S.S./Forms/C. 2118.

Army Form C. 2118

WAR DIARY
or
INTELLIGENCE SUMMARY
(Erase heading not required.)

Instructions regarding War Diaries and Intelligence Summaries are contained in F.S. Regs., Part II. and the Staff Manual respectively. Title Pages will be prepared in manuscript.

Place	Date	Hour	Summary of Events and Information	Remarks and references to Appendices
	Wednesday 25th May		Work on Secondary defences continued by parties in morning & afternoon. Route from MARTINSART to AUTHUILLE was reconnoitred as instructed. Shortly after midnight a very urgent message came from Brigade to say that 60 miners were urgently required to parade next morning at Bde Hqrs. & proceed to 179th Field Coy R.E. for work underground. Volunteers were to be taken but if necessary men must be detailed to make up their number xxxxx.	
	Thursday 26 May		Early morning Company Commanders called for volunteers & none were forthcoming. Acting on instruction among men who had previously wrought with him in Coalmines in the matter of those being no higher rate of pay from them for infantry service 60 men were detailed & marched off at 8.30 am under 2/Lieut Slorach. Later in day 30 of these were returned to Batt with a note from General Gribbon &c saying that 30 of Coy men had volunteered & the remainder to work	

1875 Wt. W593/826 1,000,000 4/15 J.B.C. & A. A.D.S.S./Forms/C. 2118.

WAR DIARY
or
INTELLIGENCE SUMMARY
(Erase heading not required.)

Army Form C. 2118

Place	Date	Hour	Summary of Events and Information	Remarks and references to Appendices
			returned to the Batln as 30 men had also volunteered for "King's Own" Rgt. and thus made up required number. Three men admitted to hospital. Work continued moving trenches at transport lines at BOUZINCOURT in afternoon. News was received to the effect that a reinforcement of 4 officers had arrived for 6th Scottish Rifles at railhead (MERICOURT) It was rumoured that at last some of the officers wounded at FESTUBERT were returning to join the Batln but this proved to be as follows :— 2/Lieut K.S. MILLER ⎫ from 4th(Extra Reserve) Batln. 2/Lieut H.R.M. CHRISTIE ⎭ Scottish Rifles 2/Lieut G.A. CRAMOND ⎫ from 13th (Service) Batln. 2/Lieut J.W. MacKINLAY ⎭ Scottish Rifles (New Army)	

Place	Date	Hour	Summary of Events and Information	Remarks and references to Appendices
	Friday 27th Aug.		Work still continued morning & afternoon. In afternoon C.O., Adj., 2nd in Comd. & Company Commanders rode up to trenches & made necessary arrangements for relieving 2/5th Lancashire Fusiliers on night of 28/29th inst. Owing to relative Strengths of Battalions the 6th Co. Rifles and 1/4th Loyal North Lancashire Regt. were together to relieve the 2/5 Lancashire Fusiliers, in same manner as tomorrow, except that on this occasion the two relieving Battalions were to change places with each other, which caused the 7th Co Rifles to be on the extreme left of the Brigade's front, joining hands with a Regiment of Gurkhas on the left. One man called Tai, stretcher attached to 1st Dep. Bde. Supply Service for pioneer duties, was admission to hospital.	

WAR DIARY
or
INTELLIGENCE SUMMARY
(Erase heading not required.)

Army Form C. 2118

Place	Date	Hour	Summary of Events and Information	Remarks and references to Appendices
	Saturday 28th Aug		Working parts only furnished in morning. At 7pm Battalion marched off by platoons to trenches, (via village of AVELUY) amid torrents of rain & a good deal of thunder & lightning. Relief was reported to be complete by about 10.30pm.	
	Sunday 29th Aug.		Few admins were to hospital today. One Sergt & 2 men returned from 179th Inniskilling Coy RE as they did not wish to remain; & have with exchanged for 1 Corpl & 2 men designs transfering. Day in the trenches very quiet. Our parties sniping except for some shelling of road behind our front line.	
	Monday 30th Aug.		Night passed quietly. Some heavy rain fell. 2/Lieut G.B. Box to admitted to hospital suffering from swollen jaw.	

WAR DIARY
or
INTELLIGENCE SUMMARY

Army Form C. 2118

Place	Date	Hour	Summary of Events and Information	Remarks and references to Appendices
Tuesday	31st Aug.		Night Quiet. Day uneventful. The enemy severely shelled the afternoon as it was appropriate time for shelling road behind trenches. Further damage to Hun cannot & Press. In evening enemy got a direct hit with shrapnel to a portion of parapet in section held by C Coy wounding one man in head and severely shaking other three men who were near at the time. These four men were sent to [crossed out] Field Ambulance.	
Wednesday	1st Sept		Night quiet except for machine gun display firing after occupation of machine guns. Day passed uneventfully. Several shells of woods. Three unrated shrapnel	References in Diary to September

51st Div⁴
121/7570

Confidential

War Diary
of
1/6th Scottish Rifles

From 1st Sept 1915 to 30th Sept 1915

Vol IV

Army Form C. 2118

WAR DIARY
or
INTELLIGENCE SUMMARY
(Erase heading not required.)

Instructions regarding War Diaries and Intelligence Summaries are contained in F. S. Regs., Part II. and the Staff Manual respectively. Title Pages will be prepared in manuscript.

Place	Date	Hour	Summary of Events and Information	Remarks, and references to Appendices
Wednesday	1st Sept.		Night quiet except for desultory firing of rifles and occasional of machine guns. Day passed uneventfully. Usual shelling of road Admitted to hospital sick.	

Army Form C. 2118

WAR DIARY
or
INTELLIGENCE SUMMARY
(Erase heading not required.)

Place	Date	Hour	Summary of Events and Information	Remarks and references to Appendices
	Thursday 2nd Sept.		Day passed quiet except for enemy shelling of wood in front our bivouacs. Sent several shells over in direction of village of OVILLERS, & some reply were made on AVELUY. Enemy sent over a few more rifle grenades. It is thought that there must be fired from a special kind of rifle capable of throwing a distance of about 300 yards. 3 men admitted to hospital wounded.	
	Friday 3rd Sept.		About 30 rifle grenades sent over during night but little damage done. Our Artillery were reported to open on the point from which it was thought they came but the result of their fire could not be observed. Lieut & Mr (?) J. HAMILTON left for 2 weeks leave to Scotland. 3 men admitted to hospital sick	

1875 Wt. W593/826 1,000,000 4/15 J.B.C. & A. A.D.S.S./Forms/C. 2118.

WAR DIARY
or
INTELLIGENCE SUMMARY

(Erase heading not required.)

Army Form C. 2118

Place	Date	Hour	Summary of Events and Information	Remarks and references to Appendices
	Saturday 4th Sept		Commanding Officer attended Conference of all C.O.s at Bde Head qrs at 2.30 to discuss points of trench routine. About 11.30 pm message received from Bde that reinforcement [draft] of 50 men would arrive next day	
	Sunday 5th Sept.		Draft of 49 other ranks reached rail head about mid-day & marched to Transport lines at BOUZINCOURT where they were billeted over night. Day passed uneventfully. One man admitted to hospital from Transport Coy. gassed.	

WAR DIARY
or
INTELLIGENCE SUMMARY

(Erase heading not required.)

Army Form C. 2118

Place	Date	Hour	Summary of Events and Information	Remarks and references to Appendices
Warloy	6th Sept.		Draft of 49 reached Battn. Headqrs. about 11 a.m. & were inspected by Medical Officer. They seemed much fatigued & many were unaccustomed to marching any distance. Seven members of the draft (including one Sergt.) have been wounded at FESTUBERT & are rejoining the Battn. the others came from the 3rd line Unit at Hamilton. As orders has been issued by the A.D.M.S. that all drafts are to be isolated & kept under medical supervision for 14 days before mixing with their unit, the party was marched back to BOUZINCOURT under 2/Lieut. R.G.M. LOUDON who was instructed to take command of them for the period & give them a course of close order drill etc. of which they appeared to stand in some need.	

WAR DIARY
or
INTELLIGENCE SUMMARY
(Erase heading not required.)

Army Form C. 2118

Place	Date	Hour	Summary of Events and Information	Remarks and references to Appendices
	Tuesday 7th Sept		Mirral came from Ordnance that a new VICKERS Machine Gun was ready for issue to the Unit; arrangements were made to draw it. This makes the 4th Machine Gun a charge. After a period of nearly 6 months Service in this Country. Such appears to be the maximum Spell with which our Country adapts itself to the conditions of war with which it has to deal. 5 men admitted to Hospital sick. Day passed without returns, incident - ! eight seemed to be heard similar than usual - Enemy working to relieve taking place in enemy's grd. Return called for number of killed + prisoners in Bn-; told their attacks + RE already + more Serving with Battalion. One man transferred sick.	
	Wednesday 8th Sept		Trench mortars again rather frequent but no damage done. Medical Officer went to BOUZINCOURT to inspect draft. Return of numbers absent to Bn as follows:- 46 with RE. Coy; 112 with Bn. Coy- One man transferred - same white with RE	

WAR DIARY
or
INTELLIGENCE SUMMARY
(Erase heading not required.)

Army Form C. 2118

Place	Date	Hour	Summary of Events and Information	Remarks and references to Appendices
	Thursday 9th Sept		Day passed uneventfully. Capt. D.L. Fray & 9 other ranks went on a motor lorry to Scotland. Weather still very fine though nights cold.	
	Friday 10th Sept		Day comparatively quiet. In afternoon Adjt. went to AVELUY to take arrangements as to taking over duties of Bt. in Bde. Reserve when the usual guards & working parties have to be furnished. The new draft was then inspected at drill in BOUZINCOURT. About 10.30 p.m. a message came from "A" Coy. in trenches that enemy had made three direct hits on parapet & had wounded two men. One proved to be a scalp wound & the other a more serious one on the Elbow. It was with difficulty that our Artillery came to personal reply. 3 men taken to hospital wounded Sick.	

WAR DIARY
or
INTELLIGENCE SUMMARY

Army Form C. 2118

Place	Date	Hour	Summary of Events and Information	Remarks and references to Appendices
	Saturday 11th Sept.		Mercer came from Bde. at 1.0 a.m. All leave suspended till further notice." Day passes merciful except for some shelling of wood in afternoon. The Bt. was relieved in trenches at 9.50 p.m. by 1/5th Lancashire Fusiliers. Letter "C" Coy. remain in support at POSTE LESBOS & Letters A B & D Coys. marched to outpost at BILLS in AVELUY which are the necessary Road Guards in vill.2e works about 11 p.m. 1/8th L'pool Regt. at 5.30 p.m. Lieut. & Qr. Mr. J. HAMILTON returned from leave. 1 man transferred sick, was been taken on fm.	
	Sunday 12th Sept.		Church parade was held at D Coy Billets at 11:30 am. 3 men admitted to hospital wounded. 1 man to hospital sick.	

WAR DIARY or INTELLIGENCE SUMMARY

Army Form C. 2118

Place	Date	Hour	Summary of Events and Information	Remarks and references to Appendices
	Monday 13th Sept		4 working parties of 20 each and one of 15 have to be furnished daily, and those kepts with mm memory for Guards amount to more than the Bn. Can find. There parties have the reserves. 3 Officers attended Bomb School for instruction. Brigade called for nominal roll of 112 miners and it seems probable that there may be withdrawn from Bn. Lut C Coy were withdrawn from support in word to Bulls- in AVELUY in evening to make room for a Company of New Army. 2nd Lieopold attended C.O. attended Conference	
	Tuesday 14 Sept		Usual working parties furnished. at Bde Hdqrs at 3 p.m at which it was decided to divert ten days to drill and Company training by way of some little preparation for any thing in the nature of a forward move that might be required of the Battalion in the near future. About 16 men attend Bomb School in AVELUY. One of these was slightly injured by accident with bomb 1 was admitted Hospital, sick.	

WAR DIARY
or
INTELLIGENCE SUMMARY
(Erase heading not required.)

Army Form C. 2118

Place	Date	Hour	Summary of Events and Information	Remarks and references to Appendices
	Wednesday 15th Sept		Companies went for run from 7 to 8 am. Breakfast at 8. the Carried out programme of markets at Drill & an close order drill in field west of Village Cemetery. 2 men admitted to hospital sick.	
	Thursday 16 Sept		Yesterday's programme of training repeated. About 12 noon Brigade a very unfortunate accident occurred at Bomb School by the accidental bursting of a bomb while a class of about 15 men belonging to the Battalion was being instructed. 91 wounded in 12 men of the Battalion being severely wounded including a Lance Sergt. who were in the personal staff of the School. It was not clear whether the accident was due to a defective bomb or to carelessness on the part of the instructor. Brigadier General Stibbert sent a personal note to Commanding Officer expressing his regret for the two casualties by the regiments in the regrettable manner.	

WAR DIARY
or
INTELLIGENCE SUMMARY
(Erase heading not required.)

Army Form C. 2118

Place	Date	Hour	Summary of Events and Information	Remarks and references to Appendices
	Friday 17th Sept		Sergt. J.H. GOLDIE has been selected to leave as an Instructor of reinforcements for a probable period of 2 months. One man admitted to hospital, sick.	
			Working parties again resumed. Lieut. "D" Coy was ordered to return to support at POSTE LES DOS at 10 a.m. on account of withdrawal of troops of New Army who has occupied a portion of the Brigade front. 3 men admitted to hospital, sick.	
	Saturday 18th Sept		Battalion was relieved in Brigade Reserve by 1/4th Loyal North Lancashire Regt. about 9.30 p.m. and Companies (including Letter "D") marched independently to billets in MARTINSART. Men received orders that every available man would be required for working parties in morning & this would be continued daily. 2 men admitted to hospital, sick wounded	Capt D.L. GRAY returned from leave having been delayed one day at Folkestone owing to Channel operations

WAR DIARY
or
INTELLIGENCE SUMMARY

(Erase heading not required.)

Army Form C. 2118

Place	Date	Hour	Summary of Events and Information	Remarks and references to Appendices
Salford	19th Sept.		Work parties to the strength of every available man paraded at Brigade Head qrs in AVELUY at 8.30 a.m. In afternoon memo received that 154th Bde. would be relieved by 152nd Bde. on night 21/22nd September. Orders for relief would be issued later, and 6th/Sco. Rif. would be located in BOUZINCOURT. In accordance with standing orders for Bn. in Div. Reserve Coy. Commanders reconnoitred route to AUTHUILLE	
			brushing partys [?]	

Army Form C. 2118

WAR DIARY
or
INTELLIGENCE SUMMARY
(Erase heading not required.)

Place	Date	Hour	Summary of Events and Information	Remarks and references to Appendices
	Monday 20th Sept		Work parties continued. Operation orders issued for move of Brigade to what is described as "rear area"	
	Tuesday 21st Sept		Capt HAY went to Bde Headrs to receive instructions regarding billeting in BOUZINCOURT. Billeting party went to latter place at 10-30 am. Battalion was relieved in MARTINSART by 1/4 Loyal North Lancashire Regt. about 7.30 pm and marched by Companies to BOUZINCOURT. Billets very good. Outline programme of Battalion Training received from Brigade for following five days including one days interbrigade.	

1875 Wt. W593/826 1,000,000 4/15 J.B.C. & A. A.D.S.S./Forms/C. 2118.

Army Form C. 2118

WAR DIARY
or
INTELLIGENCE SUMMARY
(Erase heading not required.)

Place	Date	Hour	Summary of Events and Information	Remarks and references to Appendices
Vadencourt	Wednesday 22 Sept.		General inspection of clothing boots equipment etc of Companies by Co. Adj. & Qr. Mr. All Transport less 20 Horses and a few mining vehicles was taken back to VADENCOURT WOOD a distance of about 6 miles S.W. of BOUZINCOURT. Shortage of water was given as reason for this most inconvenient arrangement.	
	Thursday 23 Sept.		Companies began day with a run from 7-8 am the followed Coy. war drill & musketry from 9.30 till 12.30 and again in afternoon from 2.30 till 4.30. About 4 pm Brigadier General Ilifford saw the Battalion at work on drill ground and appeared pleased with their movements. 2/Lieut. SLORACH rejoined Battalion after a period of four months attachment to 179th Coy R.E. during which	

WAR DIARY
or
INTELLIGENCE SUMMARY
(Erase heading not required.)

Army Form C. 2118

Place	Date	Hour	Summary of Events and Information	Remarks and references to Appendices
			time he had charge of mining operations in front trenches	
LA BOISELLE			One man admitted Stationary Hospital, SICK.	
	Friday 24th Sept.		Companies continued close order drill musketry in morning & afternoon. At 4pm a lecture was given to all ranks by Captain HARTLEY Chemical Adviser, 3rd Army, on means of protection against 'poisonous Gas' with special reference to the TUBE Pattern HELMET recently issued.	

WAR DIARY or INTELLIGENCE SUMMARY

Place: Saturday 25th Sept.

Companies carried out 1½ hours drill musketry in morning. A route march of 8 miles has been arranged for the afternoon but has to be cancelled owing to wet weather. Companies did musketry in billets instead.

In evening Brigade Operation Orders for move on night of 26/27th Sept. were received. The 151st Brigade would relieve the 152nd Brigade in trenches & works etc and the Battalion would be in Brigade Reserve and would occupy BRIDGE HEAD WORKS and SHELTERS EAST of RIVER ANCRE.

Each Battalion in Brigade would detail 10 of its best Grenadiers & be attached from Battalions the Toledos in AVELUY.

SECRET & URGENT

In evening the following message arrived from Brigade:—

" The following memo. from the Commander-in-chief has been received by the G.O.C. 3rd Army:—

WAR DIARY
or
INTELLIGENCE SUMMARY

Army Form C. 2118

Place	Date	Hour	Summary of Events and Information	Remarks and references to Appendices
			"Chief wishes troops to be informed that he feels confident that they realise how much our success in the forthcoming operations depends on the individual efforts of each officer, non-commissioned officer and man. He wishes this to be conveyed to them verbally, and in such manner as not to disclose our intentions to the enemy." G.H.Q. 11·40 a.m. 24/9/15 — This was communicated verbally to officers & men. Pnr. we admitted J. Hospital Sick.	
Sunday	26/9/4.		Church Parade in field at 10·0 a.m. At 1·0 p.m. Battalion moved off by Companies from BOUZINCOURT via MARTINSART — BOIS D'AVELUY — and AVELUY and reached its station about 2·30 p.m. Shelters were very primitive and now occupied by	

WAR DIARY
or
INTELLIGENCE SUMMARY

(Erase heading not required.)

Army Form C. 2118

Place	Date	Hour	Summary of Events and Information	Remarks and references to Appendices
	Monday 27th Sept		half Battn. while the other half occupied a recent made secondline trench about 200 yards further forward. One man admitted to hospital sick. Working parties 1 Officer 2 N.C.O.s & 28 men continue the provided every 4 hours. Day passed quietly. General Hibbert visited Bn in afternoon. In evening another working party of 1 Officer & 20 other ranks called for. There was a little rifle fire at night but no shelling. One man admitted to hospital sick.	
	Tuesday 28th Sept.		Working parties still continue & good progress is being made with the work which consists in driving seven parallel saps or tunnels at right angles to front line trench underneath our barbed wire. These are placed about 50 to 80 yards apart and each tunnel measures about 5 feet high by 3 feet wide	

WAR DIARY
or
INTELLIGENCE SUMMARY
(Erase heading not required.)

Army Form C. 2118

Place	Date	Hour	Summary of Events and Information	Remarks and references to Appendices
			Two of the men are being driven through sand & the others through clay and chalk. After going under the front parapet they are proceeding till the roof is within about one foot of the surface of the ground. About 4 p.m. orders received for Battalion to go into billets in AVELUY. Capt. HAY had difficulty in finding billets for Companies before darkness fell, but by 8 pm the Battn. less Letter "D" Company had moved to the village which was rather more comfortable for all concerned than the trenches occupied since Sunday afternoon. 2/Lieut J.W. SLORACH sent to hospital & he has not thoroughly recovered from the effects of being "gassed" whilst attached to 179th Tunnelling Coy. R.E. on mining operations. Two men admitted to hospital sick	

WAR DIARY
or
INTELLIGENCE SUMMARY

(Erase heading not required.)

Army Form C. 2118

Place	Date	Hour	Summary of Events and Information	Remarks and references to Appendices
	Wednesday 29th Sept.		Billets found for Letts "D" Coy in village. Working parties still continue night & day in reliefs of 4 hours each. One man admitted to hospital, sick.	
	Thursday 30 Sept.		Work carried on as usual. In evening enemy sent one or two shells into village, one of which wounded a man attached to Grenadier Company. 2/Lieut G.B. BAXTER sent to Field Ambulance sick. One man admitted to hospital sick, one wounded.	

Special Order of the Day.

The Field-Marshal Commanding-in-Chief has received the following message from Field-Marshal Right Hon. H.H. Earl Kitchener of Khartoum, Secretary of State for War:—

To—

27th September, 1915.

"SIR JOHN FRENCH,
General Headquarters.

My warmest congratulations to you and all serving under you on the substantial success you have achieved and my best wishes for the progress of your important operations.

KITCHENER."

1st Printing Co., R.E.   G.H.Q. 1612

121/75-70

S72/RM

Confidential

War Diary
of
1/6th Scottish Rifles

From 1st October to 31st October 1915

Vol V

WAR DIARY
or
INTELLIGENCE SUMMARY

Army Form C. 2118

Place	Date	Hour	Summary of Events and Information	Remarks and references to Appendices
Friday	1st October 1915		Work continues. Lancashire dropped in village in morning but little damage done. A Special Order of the Day was received from Secretary of State for War addressed to Field-Marshal Commanding-in-Chief in the Fires Congratulating the troops which has taken part in recent advances upon the substantial success achieved and conveying best wishes for further progress. Brigadier General G.L. HIBBERT slightly wounded by rifle bullet. Command of Brigade temporarily devolves upon Lt.Col. R.H. HINDLE, 1/4 Loyal North Lanc Rgt. Orders received for trench reliefs. The Batt. would take	
Saturday	2nd Oct.		over a section of from line trench on night of 3/4th October from 2/5th Lancashire Fusiliers - from of Coln of duty not stated. A working party under 2/Lieut MILLER was shelled while at work upon a communication trench	

WAR DIARY or INTELLIGENCE SUMMARY

Army Form C. 2118

(Erase heading not required.)

Instructions regarding War Diaries and Intelligence Summaries are contained in F. S. Regs., Part II and the Staff Manual respectively. Title Pages will be prepared in manuscript.

Place	Date	Hour	Summary of Events and Information	Remarks and references to Appendices
	Sunday 3rd Oct.		Two of the party were slightly wounded and went to Khopino. A man arrived Khopino sick. Church parade at 11.0 a.m. in fields near billets. At 2.30 p.m. Companies marched off independently to take over trenches and at 3.50 p.m. the relief of 2/S Lancashire Fusiliers by the Battalion was reported the complete. On the left of the Battn was the 8th Bn. Argyll & Sutherland Highlanders, on the right was the 1/4 & 7/2 Loyal North Lancashire Regt. 2 men admitted to hospine sick. 1 man wounded	

1875 Wt. W593/826 1,000,000 4/15 J.B.C. & A. A.D.S.S./Forms/C. 2118.

WAR DIARY
or
INTELLIGENCE SUMMARY

Place	Date	Hour	Summary of Events and Information	Remarks and references to Appendices
Monday	4th Oct		Day passed uneventfully. Hot drinks are supplied to the trenches at night & it is hoped to continue this nightly.	
Tuesday	5th October		Day passed uneventfully. 2 men admitted to hospital sick	

WAR DIARY
or
INTELLIGENCE SUMMARY

(Erase heading not required.)

Army Form C. 2118

Place	Date	Hour	Summary of Events and Information	Remarks and references to Appendices
	Wednesday 6th Oct.		Day passed uneventfully. Trench mortars occasional troublesome. 2/Lieut A.C. BAXTER returned from Machine Gun Course at WISQUES. One man admitted to hospital sick one wounded.	
	Thursday 7th Oct.		Day passed uneventfully. About 11 pm our howitzers appears to be successful in silencing a trench mortar which has been more than usually active. Command of Brigade taken over on this date by Brigadier General G.T.G. EDWARDS C.B., recently Colonel of 20th Hussars. 3 men admitted to hospital sick	

WAR DIARY
or
INTELLIGENCE SUMMARY

Army Form C. 2118

Place	Date	Hour	Summary of Events and Information	Remarks and references to Appendices
Friday	8th Oct.		Day uneventful. Machine gun fire swept road when workers filed. Sent one [officer?] to inspect & develop machine Gun Cover at WISQUES. One man admitted to hospital sick	
Saturday	9 Oct.		Tour of front line trenches made by Brig. Genl G.T.G. EDWARDS, in morning during which attention was drawn to defence points of trench nature which was considered of special importance. 3 men admitted to hospital sick.	

WAR DIARY
or
INTELLIGENCE SUMMARY

Army Form C. 2118

Place	Date	Hour	Summary of Events and Information	Remarks and references to Appendices
	Sunday 10th Oct.		Day uneventful. Artillery of both sides were pretty active about 10.15 p.m. 4 men admitted to hospital sick	
	Monday 11th Oct		Day passed without incident. In evening one man was wounded in head while passing through wood with rations to the trenches. Night comparatively quiet. 2 men admitted to hospital sick 1 man wounded	
	Tuesday 12th Oct.		About 10.30 a.m. Pioneer Sergt. J. CUTHBERTSON was shot dead through the head whilst attending to his duties in the wood. He was buried in AVELUY Cemetery in the afternoon, Major MACGIBBON Chaplain 6th Battalion officiating	

WAR DIARY
or
INTELLIGENCE SUMMARY
(Erase heading not required.)

Army Form C. 2118

Place	Date	Hour	Summary of Events and Information	Remarks and references to Appendices
	Wednesday 13th Oct.		Lieut Col. W. MARTIN KAY rejoined the Battalion today. He appears to have completely recovered from the wound he received at the FESTUBERT attack on 15th June & was most heartily welcomed back to take Command of the Regiment once more. Six men admitted to hospital sick Day passed quietly. Some shelling of wood about midday. Night very quiet.	
	Thursday 14th Oct.		Day passed uneventfully. Machine gun fire over flat oak wood was fairly active for a short time, but this was apparently our own target was well behind the front line trenches. Otherwise the night was quiet. Two men admitted to hospital sick	Captain J. LUSK went on a weeks leave to Scotland.

WAR DIARY

or

INTELLIGENCE SUMMARY

(Erase heading not required.)

Army Form C. 2118

Place	Date	Hour	Summary of Events and Information	Remarks and references to Appendices
Friday	15th Oct.		Billeting Officer and party left the trenches early this morning to obtain billets for Battalion Head Quarters and two Coys. in Brigade Reserve at AVELUY. The Garrison was quiet and about 1.30 pm the Battalion was relieved in the front line trenches by the 2/5th Lancashire Fusiliers. "A" and "B" Coys. proceeded to POSTE LESDOS where they relieved one Company of the 1/4th Royal North Lancashire Regt. in outpost. Battalion Head Quarters and "C" and "D" Coys proceeded to billets in AVELUY, and took same over about 2.30 pm without noteworthy incident. 2/Lieut J.W. MACKINLAY and four other ranks were detained to attend a case of "sniping" at SENLIS and this party left at mid-day to rejoin this. Nine N.C.O's and men rejoined the Battalion this evening from the Brigade Grenadier Coy. where they had passed the necessary tests and course	

WAR DIARY
or
INTELLIGENCE SUMMARY

(Erase heading not required.)

Army Form C. 2118

Place	Date	Hour	Summary of Events and Information	Remarks and references to Appendices
Feturday	16 Oct		entitled to wear the Grenadier's Badge. Ten NCO's and men were detailed to join the Brigade Grenadier Coy. for a course of training. Three subalters returned sick. Eighty NCO's and men from the two Companies in AVELUY were employed all day in various working parties. The two Companies at POSTE LESDOS also supplied working party of 30 NCO's and men for work in Communication trenches. There working parties will be employed each day while the Battalion is in Brigade Reserve. The enemy's artillery sent several shells into AVELUY this afternoon, but without no resulting casualties. About 7.30 pm. a message was received from the Brigade that movements in the enemy's line had been observed which indicated a possible attack on our frontage. Instructions were given as to the Battalion's part if assembly should an alarm be given, and Companies were instructed accordingly. The night however passed quietly	

WAR DIARY or INTELLIGENCE SUMMARY

(Erase heading not required.)

Army Form C. 2118

Instructions regarding War Diaries and Intelligence Summaries are contained in F.S. Regs., Part II. and the Staff Manual respectively. Title Pages will be prepared in manuscript.

Place	Date	Hour	Summary of Events and Information	Remarks and references to Appendices
Sunday	17 Oct		Working parties continued. The few men not engaged in work parties attended baths in the morning. Brigade Bath Plane Divine Service was conducted by MAJOR McGIBBON at 12 noon, but the attendance was necessarily very small. About 10 p.m. detailed instructions were issued by the Brigade regarding a new scheme of working parties to commence by 10 a.m. on 18th inst. Companies in AVELUY and in POSTE LESDOS were instructed accordingly. One man admitted to hospital sick.	
Monday	18 Oct		Working parties in terms of the new scheme was employed all day. A Lewis Gun Emplacement I was found most of the afternoon on the left, but no definite information regarding its position was obtained. No incidents worthy of report occurred. 4 men to hospital sick.	
Tuesday	19 Oct		Working parties continued. Day passed without eventful incident.	
Wednesday	20 Oct		Working parties continued. Stones on by the enemy but was out into AVELUY this that A and B Companies here done. Orders were received that A and B Companies be relieved to-morrow at POSTE LESDOS and proceed to Gillett in AVELUY with remainder of Battalion.	one man to hospital wounded
Thursday	21 Oct		Working parties continued. A & B Coys. was relieved in POSTE LESDOS about 4 p.m. and marched to billets in AVELUY.	

WAR DIARY
or
INTELLIGENCE SUMMARY
(Erase heading not required.)

Army Form C. 2118

Place	Date	Hour	Summary of Events and Information	Remarks and references to Appendices
	Friday 22nd Oct		Working parties continued. Capt. J.C.E. HAY went to village of CHIPILLY. He attaches to 1st Bedford Regt. for a course of instruction in Adjutant duties. 3 men admitted to hospital sick	
	Saturday 23rd Oct.		Work parties continued. Capt. T. LUSK returned from leave. Batt. was turned out to its alarm post at 4.10 pm by Brigade message. The time taken from receipt of message until post was manned was exactly 30 minutes. 7 men admitted to hospital sick	
	Sunday 24th Oct.		Work parties continued. Church Parade held at 11:30 at which Major MacGIBBON officiated. He told the Battn. that he has been transferred to No 23 General Hospital at ETAPLES and very much regrets leaving the Battalion	

Army Form C. 2118

WAR DIARY
or
INTELLIGENCE SUMMARY
(Erase heading not required.)

Place	Date	Hour	Summary of Events and Information	Remarks and references to Appendices
			hot which he had served for a period of six months in this country. Major MacGIBBON's services for the Battalion have in every way been most valuable and acceptable and his presence will be much missed by Officers and men alike. One man to hospital sick.	
Monday 28th Oct.			Work parties continued. A system of dealing with defaulters under Brigade arrangements was instituted by collecting all Regtl Police of Brigade in one Central Billet in village of AVELUY where all defaulters would be taken charge of but still available for Regtl fatigues if required	

Army Form C. 2118

WAR DIARY
or
INTELLIGENCE SUMMARY
(Erase heading not required.)

Place	Date	Hour	Summary of Events and Information	Remarks and references to Appendices
	Tuesday 26th Oct.		Frank Parker continued. Chaplain Captain COUTTS arrived & took up his duties with 15 attalion. Adjutant went to HeadQrs 1/5 Lancashire Fusiliers to arrange details of relief with that Batt. which takes place on afternoon of Wednesday 27th inst.	
	Wednesday 27th Oct		Battn. marched off to trenches from AVELUY at 2 pm and by 3.40 pm. had taken over 1st section of front line from 2/5th Lancashire Fusiliers. On the right flank & there are the 1/4th Royal North Lancashire Regt. and on the left flank the 1/8th Argyll Sutherland Highlanders (152nd Inf. Bde.) Night passed quiet. Three admitted Hospital sick.	

WAR DIARY
or
INTELLIGENCE SUMMARY

Army Form C. 2118

Place	Date	Hour	Summary of Events and Information	Remarks and references to Appendices
	Thursday 28th Oct.		Day passed comparatively quietly.	
	Friday 29th Oct.	7.30 am	From 7.30 am enemy artillery and trench mortars were specially active. It is estimated that during this period about 400 shells of different kinds reached our lines and while doing little or no damage to the portion of line held by the Battalion about 80 yards of front line trench in portion held by 1st Loyal North Lancashire Regt was completely destroyed. Artillery retaliation could only be secured by our Artillery.	

WAR DIARY
or
INTELLIGENCE SUMMARY

(Erase heading not required.)

Army Form C. 2118

Instructions regarding War Diaries and Intelligence Summaries are contained in F. S. Regs., Part II. and the Staff Manual respectively. Title Pages will be prepared in manuscript.

Place	Date	Hour	Summary of Events and Information	Remarks and references to Appendices
			of about half a dozen rounds, and that after considerable pause in the part of the Infantry. It is to be observed that such tactics and attempts inadequate support on the part of our Artillery two a very pointless effect on the moral of the troops in the trenches and cannot fail to induce in the Enemy a feeling of superiority which it is very undesirable that he should possess. In the afternoon our artillery bombarded the enemy's lines in a somewhat slapdash scheme, a time table of which was furnished to the Infantry for their information. The number of rounds fired was again very limited and so far as could be observed from our lines the results were not very encouraging.	

1875 Wt. W593/826 1,000,000 4/15 J.B.C. & A. A.D.S.S./Forms/C. 2118.

WAR DIARY
or
INTELLIGENCE SUMMARY

(Erase heading not required.)

Army Form C. 2118

Place	Date	Hour	Summary of Events and Information	Remarks and references to Appendices
	Saturday 30th Oct.		In the evening a neighbouring battalion Brigade HQ arranged an intricate scheme of rifle & machine gun fire which due notice was given to this Unit. It made up in elaborateness of detail what it lacked in effectiveness, and undoubtedly failed to impress the enemy. Six men admitted to hospital sick, & one man wounded.	
			In morning Enemy again bombarded Post of Royal North Lancs trench which shook the edge of our Lats on Brigade arranged for a working party 1/8th Royal Scots to come up & assist in repairing damage done to trenches and wire. This party did good work. Two men admitted to hospital sick.	

Army Form C. 2118

WAR DIARY
or
INTELLIGENCE SUMMARY
(Erase heading not required.)

Instructions regarding War Diaries and Intelligence Summaries are contained in F. S. Regs., Part II and the Staff Manual respectively. Title Pages will be prepared in manuscript.

Place	Date	Hour	Summary of Events and Information	Remarks and references to Appendices
	Sunday 31st Oct.		Day passed uneventfully. Occasional shelling of roads and trenches. Rain incessant. 4 men admitted to hospital sick 2 — wounded.	

Special Order of the Day.

The Field-Marshal Commanding-in-Chief has received the following message from His Majesty The King:—

To—

"Field-Marshal SIR JOHN FRENCH,
   Commander-in-Chief,
      British Expeditionary Force.   30th September, 1915.

I heartily congratulate you and all ranks of my Army under your command upon the success which has attended their gallant efforts since the commencement of the combined attack.

I recognise that this strenuous and determined fighting is but the prelude to greater deeds and further victories.

I trust the sick and wounded are doing well.

GEORGE, R.I."

The following reply has been sent:—

To—

"HIS MAJESTY THE KING,
   Buckingham Palace.   1st October, 1915.

Your Majesty's Forces in France are deeply grateful for your Majesty's most gracious message AAA There is no sacrifice the troops are not prepared to make to uphold the honour and traditions of your Majesty's Army and to secure final and complete victory.

J. D. P. FRENCH,
   Field-Marshal."

1st Printing Co., R E. G.H.Q. 1639

Special Order of the Day.

By Field-Marshal SIR J. D. P. FRENCH, G.C.B., O.M., G.C.V.O., K.C.M.G.,
Commander-in-Chief, British Army in the Field.

The Field-Marshal Commanding-in-Chief desires to express to Brigadier-General H. M. Trenchard, C.B., D.S.O., A.D.C., and all ranks of the Royal Flying Corps, his appreciation of the valuable work they have performed during the battle which commenced on the 25th September. He recognises the extremely adverse weather conditions which entailed flying under heavy fire at very low altitudes. He desires especially to thank pilots and observers for their plucky work in co-operation with the artillery, in photography and the bomb attacks on the enemy's railways, which were of great value in interrupting his communications. Throughout these operations the Royal Flying Corps have gallantly maintained the splendid record they have achieved since the commencement of the campaign.

J. D. P. FRENCH, Field-Marshal,
Commander-in-Chief,
British Army in the Field.

4th October, 1915.

1st Printing Co., R.E. G.H.Q. 1659

1/6th Servian Rifles
Nov – Dec. 1915
Vol VI

121/7954

9.P.
33 sheet

WAR DIARY
or
INTELLIGENCE SUMMARY

(Erase heading not required.)

Army Form C. 2118

1/6" Scottish Rifles

Place	Date	Hour	Summary of Events and Information	Remarks and references to Appendices
	Monday 1st Nov. 1915		Still raining. Day passed without incident of interest. Trenches very bad. 5 men admitted to hospital sick.	
	Tuesday 2nd Nov. 1915		Rain still continues. Working parties engaged in construction of new shelters in front line. Were instructed to assist in repairing damage done to trench walls by heavy rains. Communication trenches in especially bad state. Revision holes in some places are foot & eighteen inches deep filled with mud and water, and in some posts of the front trench work. Stakes and planks were floating about.	4 men admitted to hospital sick & one wounded

WAR DIARY
or
INTELLIGENCE SUMMARY

Army Form C. 2118

Place	Date	Hour	Summary of Events and Information	Remarks and references to Appendices
	Wednesday 3rd Nov.		Day dry & sunny & the change much appreciated. 1/4th Loyal North Lancs. on our right reported 2 men killed & 3 wounded by a chance shell.	
	Thursday 4th Nov.		Occasional shelling of road. 10 men another batch sick.	

WAR DIARY
or
INTELLIGENCE SUMMARY

(Erase heading not required.)

Army Form C. 2118

Place	Date	Hour	Summary of Events and Information	Remarks and references to Appendices
	Friday 5th Nov.		Work parties furnished for troops other than the Garrison of lines. For work on Communication trenches and support line. 5 men admitted hospital sick 2 " " " wounded	
	Saturday 6th Nov.		In morning a memo was received through Brigade Hdqrs from 51st Division that the undermentioned officer has been awarded a French decoration as stated:— Chevalier 5th Class Legion of Honour Captain J. LUSK 1/6 Bn. The Cameronians It was notified that the Army Commander would present this decoration personally at ACHEUX on Sunday 7th November and instructions were issued that Captain	

WAR DIARY
or
INTELLIGENCE SUMMARY

Army Form C. 2118

J. LUSK to detailed to attend at 11. am.
Late at night news was received from Brigade that Bletchley office was to send to Heilly 5th Dorset Highlanders at village of HENENCOURT at 10.15 am Sunday morning and that trench stores were near the road for handing over at 10.30 am Sunday. This appears as if a relief was about to take place though such has not definitely stated.

5 men admitted to hospital sick.

WAR DIARY
INTELLIGENCE SUMMARY

Place	Date	Hour	Summary of Events and Information	Remarks and references to Appendices
	Sunday 7th Nov.		At about 7.30am Operation Order for move & notice of intended relief and for move was received. 154th Inf Brigade were to relieve Dales was received. The Battalion together with the 1/4th Loyal North Lancashire Regt. would be relieved that evening by 5th Seaforth Highlanders, and which had to return to shoes with the 1/4th Royal Lancashire Regt. ("King's Own") Guides from adjoining Battns were to be at West end of AVELUY at 3.15pm to take in relieving troops. In accordance with orders received yesterday Captain J. LUSK left trenches at 9 a.m. & proceeded to ACHEUX a small village 5 or 6 miles back, where	

Army Form C. 2118

WAR DIARY
or
INTELLIGENCE SUMMARY
(Erase heading not required.)

Place	Date	Hour	Summary of Events and Information	Remarks and references to Appendices
			Headqrs of 4th Division were situated in company with other eight officers of the Third Army. He was presented by General Sir E.H.H. ALLENBY K.C.B. Commanding Third Army, with the 2nd decoration, stated and returned to trenches about 3.30 pm.

At 5.25 pm relief of trenches was reported complete and Battalion marched off — reaching HENENCOURT at 9 pm. Billets were quite satisfactory most of the men being provided with rough beds and hutches of wood frame and wire netting, which was much more comfortable than lying on the floor of the barns occupied. Sick men admitted to hospital. | |

WAR DIARY
or
INTELLIGENCE SUMMARY

Army Form C. 2118

Place	Date	Hour	Summary of Events and Information	Remarks and references to Appendices
	Monday 8th Nov.		Day spent chiefly in Company inspection for the purpose of making good trenches defences after a tour of trenches. At 4.45pm all officers attended at Brigade Headqrs where a lecture was delivered by Lt. Colonel Jan Stewart 57th Div C. Staff upon the principles of attack in trench warfare.	
	Tuesday 9th Nov.		Battalion inspected by Commanding Officer. Heavy rains stating that big adv Somme would inspect Batt n 10 th inst at 11 am adjacent to Billets in convenient place. 2 men admitted to hospital sick	

Army Form C. 2118

WAR DIARY
or
INTELLIGENCE SUMMARY
(Erase heading not required.)

Place	Date	Hour	Summary of Events and Information	Remarks and references to Appendices
	Wednesday 10th Nov.		Inspection of Baggage & Horses. Exercise cancelled owing to heavy rain. Corps did work in Billets. Machine Gun Section and Bombers trained under their own Officers. 2 men admitted to hospital sick.	
	Thursday 11th Nov.		Heavy rain in morning. In afternoon rain ceased and Batt. marched to neighbouring village of MILLENCOURT and practiced a trench attack on principles laid down in Lecture on 8th inst. Intimation also received that leave for British O. was stopped. 12 O.R. was affected. One Officer and 15 other ranks.	

1875. Wt. W593/826 1,000,000 4/15 J.B.C. & A. A.D.S.S./Forms/C. 2118.

WAR DIARY
or
INTELLIGENCE SUMMARY
(Erase heading not required.)

Army Form C. 2118

Place	Date	Hour	Summary of Events and Information	Remarks and references to Appendices
	Friday 12th Nov.		Bath. worked & MILLENCOURT at 9. a.m. & again practised a trench attack after inspection by Brigadier as ordered by Brig who he was on yesterday. Rain again. Cannot inspection to be cancelled, but the attack was nevertheless carried out. Footrace play in afternoon with "Kings own" Regt. One man admitted stationary hospital, sick.	
	Saturday 13th Nov.		Working part. absorbing all available men except Machine gun Section was ordered in 3 parties of 10 & 8 men & 50 men each to and parts of 10.8ffm and 25 men. These parties marched off & struck tents at 6 a.m. & did not return till abt 6 p.m. CO Adv. advanced conference at Bde Headqrs.	

Place	Date	Hour	Summary of Events and Information	Remarks and references to Appendices
	Sunday 14th Nov		It was learned that the Brigade would take over a new line of trenches (& left of post previously held) on Tuesday night 16/17th Inst. Two men admitted to hospital sick. Church Parade at 10.30 a.m. Hall at Pte. Hqrs. At 12 noon CO. inspected kits & billets of Battalion.	
	Monday 15th Nov		Companies did work in Billets owing to rain. CO. Adj. Coy Commanders Intelligence Officer, Bombing Officer & Machine Gun Officer rode over to AUTHUILLE & thence to trenches to be taken over to know necessary arrangements.	

Place	Date	Hour	Summary of Events and Information	Remarks and references to Appendices
	Tuesday 16th Nov.		Snow lay thick upon the ground. "Antifrostbite Grease" had been issued to the Battalion and in accordance with orders received the feet and legs of every NCO & man were treated with it, and a difficult to the effect was rendered to Brigade Headqrs before marching off. Machine guns moved off about 10 am and at 4 pm the Battalion marched off to Enchess via MILLENCOURT — ALBERT — AVELUY — AUTHUILLE a total distance of about 7½ miles. Men were heavy laden with fur coats, blanket, waterproof sheet, etc in addition to the packs with usual kit. The evening was cold and misty and the roads were heavy with snow and mud. AUTHUILLE was reached about 6.45 pm when guides were waiting from 7th Gordon Highlanders who were the relieved	"

WAR DIARY
or
INTELLIGENCE SUMMARY

(Erase heading not required.)

Army Form C. 2118

Place	Date	Hour	Summary of Events and Information	Remarks and references to Appendices
			By 8.30 pm a report was sent to Brigade that relief was completed. The night had closed and a bright thrown party keeps the relief to be swiftly carried out. The 1/4 Royal Scots to Right ("King's Own") were on the right and the 1/8th Liverpool (Irish) Regt were on the left. Three Coys: A, B, & C, occupied the front line and D Coy was in support about 100 to 150 yards behind the front line. No fewer than 10 saps run out from the front to project for a distance of about 30 yards towards the enemy's lines. The front held by the three front Companies measures about 450 yards and this is held by a strength of about 195 rifles giving about 2½ yards for rifle. In afternoon Captain J. BOYD and Lieut A.C. STEWART who went round inspecting the May as 1st June reports Batt:— accompanied by 2/Lieut. W.R. CAMPBELL for 3/6 H.R.	6 men admitted to hospital sick

Army Form C. 2118

WAR DIARY
or
INTELLIGENCE SUMMARY
(Erase heading not required.)

Place	Date	Hour	Summary of Events and Information	Remarks and references to Appendices
	Wednesday 17th Nov.		Between 10 and 11.30 am enemy shells landed just behind front line knocking down portions of them but doing no damage otherwise. Night was to clear out and repairs to parados in front of parapet or tramway. 3 men admitted to hospital sick.	
	Thursday 18th Nov.		Day passed quietly. In afternoon A Coy and D Coy changed places. In evening Captain T.H. CAMPBELL and 15 other ranks went to leave to Scotland, for a week. In evening A Coy went to support and D Coy moved to front trench. 3 men admitted to hospital sick.	

WAR DIARY
or
INTELLIGENCE SUMMARY

(Erase heading not required.)

Army Form C. 2118

Place	Date	Hour	Summary of Events and Information	Remarks and references to Appendices
	Friday 19th Nov		An Artillery shoot arranged for 1.30pm has to be postponed owing to mist which made observation impossible. Men have been provided with hot drink, either soup or cocoa, each night in their churn and it is greatly appreciated, especially by Sentries on listening posts. One man admitted to hospital sick.	
	Saturday 20th Nov		Commanding Officer attended Conference at Brigade Headqrs at MARTINSART at 12 noon when points of trench routine were discussed. B Coy went to support trench & A Coy took trenches. The village of AUTHUILLE was shelled in the early afternoon and one man of the Royal North Lancs was killed. One man admitted to hospital sick.	

Place	Date	Hour	Summary of Events and Information	Remarks and references to Appendices
	Sunday 21st Nov.		nights still cold but very clear and light. Day passed quiet. Night uneventful save for occasional bursts of machine gun & rifle fire about midnight and about 3 am. In evening 2/Lieut. G. SHEARER joined the Battn. from the 3rd/6th Scottish Rifles, and was taken right up to trenches and posted to "B" Coy. One man admitted to hospital sick with grenade wound in hand.	
	" "		" "	
	Monday 22nd Nov.		Day foggy & little firing going on. Night comparatively quiet. Inverness C Coy S West transport trench and B Coy to front line. One man admitted hospital sick.	

WAR DIARY
or
INTELLIGENCE SUMMARY

Army Form C. 2118

Place	Date	Hour	Summary of Events and Information	Remarks and references to Appendices
	Tuesday 23rd Nov.		Day passed uneventfully. Arrangements for Trench Mortar and rifle grenade fire scheme which were made to take place at 11 am had to be cancelled owing to fog. In evening Captain J.C.E. HAY rejoined Battn. from Adjutants course of instruction with 1st Bedford Regt. near BRAY. He has spent period of one month instruction.	
	Wednesday 24th Nov.		In morning Capt. J.C.E. HAY took over command of "A" Coy. The trench mortar fire scheme arranged for yesterday was carried out at 11 a.m. The shooting, as far as it could be observed from our front line trench was effective, and	

WAR DIARY
or
INTELLIGENCE SUMMARY

(Erase heading not required.)

Army Form C. 2118

Place	Date	Hour	Summary of Events and Information	Remarks and references to Appendices
			provoked a certain amount of retaliation on front trenches and a volley of AUTHUILLE 2/Lieut H.R.M. CHRISTIE went to QUERRIEU in afternoon for course of instruction in telescopic sights. In evening B. Coy went to support an C Coy to front line. 2/Lieut K.S. MILLER went to hospital suffering from influenza.	
Thursday 25th Nov.			In morning some artillery fire could be heard going on in distance. Day passed uneventfully. Wind cold. 2/Lieut SPEIRS and 18 other ranks went on a week's leave to Scotland	
Friday 26th Nov			Fire Scheme carried out in morning commencing at 10 am. Enemy retaliated by sending 15 or 20 shells into AUTHUILLE immediately carrying away the chimney & a portion of the roof of the house occupied as Batt. Head.	

WAR DIARY
or
INTELLIGENCE SUMMARY
(Erase heading not required.)

Army Form C. 2118

Place	Date	Hour	Summary of Events and Information	Remarks and references to Appendices
	Saturday 27th Nov		In evening A Coy went into Support trench and D Coy into front line. Nº 14 hand Companies of Dismtd. or was admits stationary site. Commanding officer went to Bde Headqrs at MARTINSART & Conference on points of trench Routine etc. Orders were received that the Battalion would be relieved in trenches on the night of Sunday 28th inst. by 1/8th Argyll & Sutherland Highlanders and would march & billet in vicinity of HENENCOURT which were occupied when last out of trenches.	
	Sunday 28th Nov		Billeting Party consisting of Captain J. BOYD and officer for Company and the Company Qr. Mr. Sergts. Set out for HENEN COURT at about 8 a.m.	

Army Form C. 2118

WAR DIARY
or
INTELLIGENCE SUMMARY

(Erase heading not required.)

Instructions regarding War Diaries and Intelligence Summaries are contained in F. S. Regs., Part II. and the Staff Manual respectively. Title Pages will be prepared in manuscript.

Place	Date	Hour	Summary of Events and Information	Remarks and references to Appendices
Monday	29th Nov		Relief was complete at 7.45 pm and Companies marched independently — the last reliefs reaching HENENCOURT about 10.15 pm	
			Day spent in Company inspections and compiling returns indents for deficiencies etc.	
Tuesday	30th Nov.		In morning Companies carried out programme of drill — and route marches for about 2 hours.	

Abraham
Major

1875 Wt. W593/826 1,000,000 4/15 J.B.C. & A. A.D.S.S./Forms/C. 2118.

WAR DIARY
or
INTELLIGENCE SUMMARY

Army Form C. 2118

1/6 Scottish Rifles

Place	Date	Hour	Summary of Events and Information	Remarks and references to Appendices
	Wednesday 1st Decr.		In morning Companies carried out programme of Close order drill followed by a practice attack. Class laid down by Divisional in hutsin with Barbed wire entanglements. Companies Co-operating. In afternoon 2/Lieut J.W. McKINLAY went to be attached to 1st CHESHIRE Regt. for course of instruction in Adjutants duties.	
	Thursday 2nd Decr.		In morning the Battn: practised the attack at trenches west of village of MILLENCOURT with Bombers and machine gun teams. In afternoon 2/Lieut J.W. SLORACH and 15 other ranks went on 9 days leave to Britain	

WAR DIARY or INTELLIGENCE SUMMARY

Army Form C. 2118

Place	Date	Hour	Summary of Events and Information	Remarks and references to Appendices
	Friday 3rd Dec.		Battalion furnished work parties. The strength of 3 officers and 150 other ranks which started from HENENCOURT for Frechen in Buses at 7.30 am. Bombers and Machine Gun Section trained in Billets under their own Officers. In the evening Capt. J. LUSK was summoned to Brigade Head Quarters to undertake Brigade Major's duties during the latter's absence on leave. Capt. J.C.E. HAY took over the duties of Adjutant during Capt. LUSK's absence.	
	Saturday 4th Dec.		Owing to the rainy weather conditions, Companies spent the forenoon engaged in musketry etc. in Billets instead of Route marching as originally intended. During the day orders were received instructing the Battalion to relieve the 7th Gordon Highlanders in Brigade Reserve at AVELUY tomorrow — the Brigade taking over the trenches in front. In the evening Divisional Service was held.	
	Sunday 5th Dec.		Battalion marched from HENENCOURT at 2 p.m. & relieved 7th Gordon Highlanders in Brigade Reserve at AVELUY. Relief was completed by 5.30 pm.	

WAR DIARY
or
INTELLIGENCE SUMMARY
(Erase heading not required.)

Army Form C. 2118

Place	Date	Hour	Summary of Events and Information	Remarks and references to Appendices
	Monday 6th Dec.		All available men were engaged today in working parties - repairing the front line trenches or working at the R.E. Dept. In the afternoon some Officers and "C" and "D" Companies were taken over to other billets to make room for Joint Companies of the Battalions in the front line, who had been relieved by the Companies of the 7th M.L.F. On turning Junfain. About 4 p.m. Jack-Shells were dropped in the village by the Germans but the damage worthy note was done.	
	Tuesday 7th Dec.		All available men began in various working parties. The village was shelled by the Germans about mid day and again about 8.30 p.m. One of "A" Coy. billets was hit but no casualties resulted	
	Wednesday 8th Dec.		Working parties as usual Village again shelled resulting in one slight casualty in 7th Royal Lancaster Regt. Orders received in the evening that two Companies to detail to relieve one Company 2/5th Lancashire Fusiliers in F2 and orders for "A" and "C" Coys. were detailed to carry out relief tomorrow afternoon	
	Thursday 9th Dec.		Small working party employed during forenoon. "A" & "C" Coys. took over trenches in F2 and billets employees relief by 3.40 p.m. 2 & Coy. 2/5th Lancashire Fusiliers entered billets in AVELUY, and a came across taking command and Lt. Col. W. M. KAY. All aiddle men engaged on work party from 8 p.m. to 10 p.m.	

WAR DIARY
or
INTELLIGENCE SUMMARY

(Erase heading not required.)

Army Form C. 2118

Place	Date	Hour	Summary of Events and Information	Remarks and references to Appendices
Engayo 10th December			Working parties were again supplied during the day and at night from 6 p.m. to 10 p.m. About 1 p.m. the enemy shelled the village. One shell burst outside "B" Coy's billet and four men were slightly wounded.	
Saturday 11 Dec			All available men again employed on working parties. During the afternoon the village was very heavily shelled, the formerly billets had no casualties resulting. About 9 p.m. occupying by heavy artillery fire was opened by the enemy; the front lines, AVELUY, MARTINSART and ALBERT were all the targets of the enemy's guns. Considerable damage was done to the village, and one man was killed and two wounded who were with our two Companies in the front line. It is estimated that over one hundred shells were fired on to AVELUY alone during the afternoon and night.	
Sunday 12 Dec			Divine Service was held in the village at 11·30 am. During the service information was received that artillery retaliation by the enemy was anticipated on the village. The Service was therefore	

1875 Wt. W593/826 1,000,000 4/15 J.B.C. & A. A.D.S.S./Forms/C. 2118.

WAR DIARY
or
INTELLIGENCE SUMMARY

Army Form C. 2118

Place	Date	Hour	Summary of Events and Information	Remarks and references to Appendices
	Monday 13th Decr.		brought to a close and the men ordered to take shelter in the Company extemp shelter. No news the enemy opened fire shelling the village. In evening Capt J. LUSK rejoined Battalion on arrival of Brigade Major from leave.	
			Usual work, fatigues furnished. B and D Coys relieved A & C Companies in front line trenches & A & C withdrew to Billets —	
	Tuesday 14th Decr.		Usual work parties furnished.	

WAR DIARY
or
INTELLIGENCE SUMMARY

Place	Date	Hour	Summary of Events and Information	Remarks and references to Appendices
	Wednesday 15th Dec.		Usual trench parties furnished.	
	Thursday 16th Dec.		Coy 2 Coy Battalion was relieved in Brigade Reserve by 1/8 Argyll & Sutherland Highlanders at 4.30 pm and proceeded to rest billets at HENENCOURT. "B" & "D" Coys in fire trench were also relieved later in evening & they also marched in afterwards to HENENCOURT which was reached about 9.30 pm. The Battn occupied same billets as formerly. Capt. J.C.E. HAY went to Brigade Headqrs to carry out duties of Staff Captain during that officers absence on leave.	

WAR DIARY
or
INTELLIGENCE SUMMARY

(Erase heading not required.)

Army Form C. 2118

Instructions regarding War Diaries and Intelligence Summaries are contained in F. S. Regs., Part II. and the Staff Manual respectively. Title Pages will be prepared in manuscript.

Place	Date	Hour	Summary of Events and Information	Remarks and references to Appendices
	Friday 17th Decr.		Day occupied by Coy inspection & remedying necessary to complete deficiencies.	
	Saturday 18th Decr		Work party of 1 Officer and 50 other ranks detailed by Brigade & report at AVELUY at 8.30am for work in trenches. Remainder of Battn carried out Close order Drill & entrenching.	
	Sunday 19th Decr.		Church Parade and Commanding Officers Inspection of Billets and Kits. Same strength of work party furnished.	

Place	Date	Hour	Summary of Events and Information	Remarks and references to Appendices
	Monday 20th Decr		Usual work parts. Entrenching and Close order drill carried out by remainder.	
	Tuesday 21st Decr.	2.30pm	At 2.30pm Coys marched off independently to take over line of trenches in G.I.O Subsection near AUTHUILLE Route was via Trélins :- HENENCOURT - MILLENCOURT - ALBERT - AVELUY - AUTHUILLE. - AUTHUILLE was reached at 5.30pm and the line of trench was taken over at 7pm. Disposition of Coys were as follows :- A, B & C Coys in fire trench and D in support. In spite of recent rain these trenches were not in such a bad condition as was expected	

Army Form C. 2118

WAR DIARY
or
INTELLIGENCE SUMMARY
(Erase heading not required.)

Instructions regarding War Diaries and Intelligence Summaries are contained in F. S. Regs., Part II. and the Staff Manual respectively. Title Pages will be prepared in manuscript.

Place	Date	Hour	Summary of Events and Information	Remarks and references to Appendices
	Wednesday 22nd Decr		Night passed quietly. Day was wet and uncomfortable. Ammunition and stores were adjusted to Brigade Establishment as far as possible.	
	Thursday 23rd Decr	11 noon	Commanding officer attended Conference at Brigade Headqrs at 11 noon and afterwards proceeded on leave to Scotland. Major A.G. Graham took over command of Battn in his absence. Day wet and trenches very muddy. Additional pumps were brought up to rest trench. All men in support Coy were employed on front line trench. Lit by day and by night.	

1875 Wt. W593/826 1,000,000 4/15 J.B.C. & A. A.D.S.S./Forms/C. 2118.

WAR DIARY
or
INTELLIGENCE SUMMARY
(Erase heading not required.)

Army Form C. 2118

Place	Date	Hour	Summary of Events and Information	Remarks and references to Appendices
	Friday 24th Dec		Not much firing on either side during night. Owing to continuous rain, sides of trenches were continually falling in as taking the strength of the garrison of the church. In afternoon an Artillery shoot was carried out with apparent success so far as gas-effects over to observe Relativity took place at the same time & villages of [illegible] but heavily shelled.	
AUTHUILLE	Saturday 25th Dec		Artillery very active on either side. Enemy sent over a large number of Mortars Rifle Grenades, and "Oil Cans". Captain & Adjutant Jas. Rusk was buried and severely wounded by the bursting of an "Oil Can". The Brigadier-General called this morning and complimented the Battalion on the condition of the trenches, and the amount of work done since taking over this sector. Duties of Acting Adjutant were taken over by 2nd Lieut. R. Speirs.	A.

Army Form C. 2118

WAR DIARY
or
INTELLIGENCE SUMMARY
(Erase heading not required.)

Instructions regarding War Diaries and Intelligence Summaries are contained in F. S. Regs., Part II. and the Staff Manual respectively. Title Pages will be prepared in manuscript.

Place	Date	Hour	Summary of Events and Information	Remarks and references to Appendices
Sunday.	26th Dec.		All Artillery very quiet. Enemy sent over a large number of "Oil Cans" and Rifle Grenades, otherwise very quiet. Draft of 150 Other Ranks joined the Battn. from 2/6th Scottish Rifles, 3/6th Scottish Rifles and 8th H.L.I. Weather very unsettled.	
Monday.	27th Dec.		Enemy sent over several shells into AUTHUILLE in the early hours of the morning, but did no damage. Quiet during the day & exceptionally quiet at night. Weather much better. Large work parties assisted the Coys in trenches, and a very considerable amount of work was carried out on Fire Trench and Communication Trenches.	
Tuesday.	28th Dec.		Our Artillery carried out a "shoot" this afternoon, assisted by our Trench Mortars, which seemed successful, the enemy retaliated with a few shells in AUTHUILLE, but did no damage.	

WAR DIARY
or
INTELLIGENCE SUMMARY
(Erase heading not required.)

Army Form C. 2118

Place	Date	Hour	Summary of Events and Information	Remarks and references to Appendices
Wednesday	29th Dec.		This day has been very quiet. Weather good. 1/4th Loyal North Lancs. Regt. relieved this Battn. in front line trenches, & this Battn. took over that Battn's billets in AUTHUILLE. News received this morning of the death from wounds received on Christmas Day of Capt. & Adj. James Luck at the South Midland Clearing Station, Amiens, on 28th Dec.	
Thursday	30th Dec.		The day passed quietly. The enemy put a few shells into AUTHUILLE about 11.30 p.m., but did no damage. A working party from this Battn. assisted the 1/4th Loyal North Lancs. Regt. in fire trench. 2 Officers + 12 other ranks proceeded on leave to Scotland. Major Graham, Capt. Campbell + party of 20 NCOs men proceeded to Amiens to attend the funeral of the late Capt. + Adj. J. Luck.	
Friday	31st Dec.		Weather unsettled. Our Artillery carried out a shoot this afternoon. Enemy did not retaliate. About 11 p.m. enemy machine guns were busy, there was also rapid fire. Again about midnight, there was a considerable amount of rapid fire. A. Graham Major	

51ST DIVISION
154TH INFY BDE

1-6TH BN SCOTTISH RIFLES
(CAMERONIANS)
JAN-FEB 1916

51ST DIVISION
154TH INFY BDE

10 P.
14 sheets

51 1/6: Sestini Rpt.
Jan 1916.
Vol. VII

Army Form C. 2118.

WAR DIARY
or
INTELLIGENCE SUMMARY.

1/6" Scottish Rifles.

(Erase heading not required.)

Instructions regarding War Diaries and Intelligence Summaries are contained in F. S. Regs., Part II. and the Staff Manual respectively. Title pages will be prepared in manuscript.

Place	Date	Hour	Summary of Events and Information	Remarks and references to Appendices
	1916.			
	Saturday 1st Jan.		This day was very quiet. Weather unsettled. By kind permission of the Brigadier-General, this Battalion was relieved of all work parties.	M.
	Sunday 2nd Jan.		Short Services were held in each of the Company's Billets, by the Chaplain this morning. This evening "A" "B" & "D" Coys were relieved by the 15th Bn. Lancashire Fusiliers, and "C" Coy. by the 16th Bn. Northumberland Fusiliers. After the relief, which was rapidly carried out, the Battalion marched back to billets in HENENCOURT.	M
	Monday 3rd Jan.		This Battalion took part in a Brigade Route March today from HENENCOURT to BEHENCOURT and afterwards proceeded to billets in BEAUCOURT. First Transport accompanied the Battn. Weather excellent every mile.	M
	Tuesday 4th Jan.		At 1.30 p.m. Battalion left BEAUCOURT for rest billets at CARDONNETTE arriving there at 4.15 p.m.	M

Army Form C. 2118.

WAR DIARY
or
INTELLIGENCE SUMMARY.
(Erase heading not required.)

Instructions regarding War Diaries and Intelligence Summaries are contained in F.S. Regs., Part II. and the Staff Manual respectively. Title pages will be prepared in manuscript.

Place	Date	Hour	Summary of Events and Information	Remarks and references to Appendices
Wednesday.	5th Jan.		The forenoon was occupied in cleaning clothing, equipment and billets. There was no parade in the afternoon. This afternoon a Riding School for Officers was held. About twenty attended. Weather dry but dull.	
Thursday.	6th Jan.		Close order drill & musketry was carried out by Companies this forenoon. No parade in afternoon. 1/8th (Irish) "King's" Liverpool Regt. severed their connection with the 154th Infy. Brigade - left this village (CARDONNETTE) for a new area. A Guide was furnished by this Batt. to guide 1/4th Seaforths from LONGUEAU to CARDONNETTE. Also guide for 1/4th Black Watch to RAINNEVILLE, 1/5th Black Watch to COISY. Weather dull.	
Friday.	7th Jan.		Close order drill & musketry carried out this forenoon. No parade in afternoon. Commanding Officer attended a Conference at 154th Infy. Bde. H.Q. this afternoon. Heavy rain fell in afternoon and evening.	

WAR DIARY
or
INTELLIGENCE SUMMARY.

(Erase heading not required.)

Army Form C. 2118.

Place	Date	Hour	Summary of Events and Information	Remarks and references to Appendices
1916	Saturday 8th Jan.		Morning Parade consisted of Physical Drill + Company Drill + a route march of about 4 miles. Route: CARDONNETTE, COISY, RENNEVILLE, CARDONNETTE. Weather good.	M.
	Sunday 9th Jan.		Church Parade was held this morning at 11 o'clock in field West side of CARDONNETTE. After Parade the Commanding Officer inspected all billets. Weather excellent.	M.
	Monday 10th Jan.		Close order Drill, Physical exercises musketry, carried out by Coy this morning and afternoon. Commanding Officer inspected billets this morning. Weather unsettled.	M.
	Tuesday 11th Jan.		Close order and Coy. drill carried out this morning. Capt Boyd, 4 Coy. Officers + 7 NCOs proceeded to FLESSELLES to arrange billets for the Batn. Riding School for Officers held in the afternoon. Weather unsettled. Capt. J.H. KEITH left the Batn to take up a post in ENGLAND. 2Lt W.M. MAXWELL joined the Batn from 3/6 Scottish Rifles.	M.

WAR DIARY
or
INTELLIGENCE SUMMARY.

(Erase heading not required.)

Army Form C. 2118.

Place	Date	Hour	Summary of Events and Information	Remarks and references to Appendices
Wednesday.	12th Jan.		This Battalion severed it's connection with the 154th Infantry Brigade and left that Brigade area for FLESSELLES. Route:- RAINNEVILLE, MONTON-VILLERS, FLESSELLES. The Battalion had the honour of being inspected, while on the march, by GENERAL SIR DOUGLAS HAIG, G.O.C. in C. British Expeditionary Force. The General congratulated the Commanding Officer (Major A.G. Graham) on the appearance and marching of the Battalion. The Battalion this day became Divisional Troops. Weather unsettled and cold.	Nil
Thursday.	13th Jan.		This day was spent in the cleaning and repairing of billets. Weather unsettled.	Nil
Friday.	14th Jan.		Coy. Officers and Sergeants attended demonstrations of wiring etc:- at the 8th Royal Scots H.Q. this morning and afternoon. Working parties from "A" & "D" Coys made a start at erecting beds for the men in these Coys billets. In the evening all Officers attended a lecture given by the Commanding Officer of the 8th Royal Scots, on the "Organisation of Infantry". 2nd Lt. A.C. Baxter and 20 other ranks proceeded today to CARDONNETTE to form part of MACHINE GUN COMPANY.	

WAR DIARY
INTELLIGENCE SUMMARY.

Army Form C. 2118.

Place	Date	Hour	Summary of Events and Information	Remarks and references to Appendices
	19/16		attached to the 154th Infy Brigade. 2nd Lt H.R.M. Christie + 20 other ranks proceeded on leave to SCOTLAND. Weather excellent but cold.	M
Saturday	15th Jany		Officers + N.C.O.s again attended at the 8th Royal Scots H.Q. for instruction in pioneer work. A lecture was also held for Officers. Lt. Col. Kay returned from leave and resumed command of the Battalion. Captain D.L. Gray took up post of acting Adjutant. Weather very unsettled.	M
Sunday	16th Jany		Church Parade was held this morning at 10 a.m. in field at the North end of FLESSELLES. 2/Lieuts W.S. MITCHELL and J.W. MUIRHEAD joined the Battalion from 3/6th Scottish Rifles and were posted to "B" and "C" Coys respectively. Weather very unsettled.	
Monday	17th Jany		The Battalion commenced work on the new "show" trenches planned by the General Staff, 51st Division. The trenches are situated at the South end of FLESSELLES, and intended to show all the devices and tricks discovered since	

Army Form C. 2118.

WAR DIARY
or
INTELLIGENCE SUMMARY.
(Erase heading not required.)

Place	Date	Hour	Summary of Events and Information	Remarks and references to Appendices
	Monday 17th Jany 1916		Commencement of the week. 2 Companies were engaged in the usual Company work. The other 2 Companies carried out the usual Company training. Information was received to-day that CAPTAIN J.C.E HAY. had been appointed Staff Captain to 144th Bgde dated 9/1/16. The following names of officers and men of the Battalion were mentioned in Sir J. D. P. French Despatch dated 1/1/16:- Major A.A Graham, Captain J Inch, Captain St Grey, Captain J.C.E Hay, No 2454 Pte J.R. Brown No 15754 Pte W Kennah No 99 and No 2511 Pte F. Williamson. Weather very wet and unsettled.	
	Tuesday 18th Jany		C and D Companies were engaged in the morning in work on "Show Ground" trenches while A and B Companies carried out Company training. In the afternoon the weather being very wet all officers and sergeants attended a Lecture by Captain INCH 1/8 Royal Scots on Pedrail Work. All officers attended a conference held	

Army Form C. 2118.

WAR DIARY
or
INTELLIGENCE SUMMARY.
(Erase heading not required.)

Instructions regarding War Diaries and Intelligence Summaries are contained in F.S. Regs., Part II. and the Staff Manual respectively. Title pages will be prepared in manuscript.

Place	Date	Hour	Summary of Events and Information	Remarks and references to Appendices
	1916			
	Tuesday 18th Jany		at Battalion Headqrs, when the Commanding Officer congratulated Major A.G. Graham on winning the Military Cross. The weather was very wet and unsettled.	JG
	Wednesday 19th Jany		O. & B. Coys were at work on the Show Ground trenches while C. & D. Coys carried out Company training. The afternoon was observed as a holiday. The Battalion Football team played a match against the 7/8 Royal Scots. The Commandant Comdg. 1st Inf. Bde. Major General Stewart came and saw the game. The weather was very fine and clear.	JG
	Thursday 20th Jany		Companies were again engaged in ragging trenches on the "Show Ground" and carrying out Company training. In the afternoon the 13th Corps Commander General Congreve inspected the 1st line transport of the Battalion. The R.O. and its transport officer were again in attendance. The weather was again fine and clear.	JG

2353 Wt. W3541/1454 700,000 5/15 D.D.&L.   A.D.S.S./Form/C. 2118.

WAR DIARY or INTELLIGENCE SUMMARY

Army Form C. 2118.

Place	Date	Hour	Summary of Events and Information	Remarks and references to Appendices
Friday	1916 21st Jany		The Battalion commenced work at Roadmaking in the village of MONTONVILLERS. The accommodation of the Divisional area has to be doubled before 31st January and the Battalion has been made responsible for the village. Work on the Show Ground Trenches was interfered by A & B Coys. The Commanding Officer handed over to the Divisional Commander and discussed to the affairs of the Battalion. The weather was dull but dry.	29
Saturday	22nd Jany		The Companies were again engaged on work at MONTON VILLERS and on the Show Ground at the Trenches. Jackson rejoined the Battalion from the Divisional Grenade School. The weather was unsettled and wet.	29
Sunday	23rd Jany		The Battalion attended a joint Church Parade with the 1/8 the Rattan Royal Scots and Divisional Headquarters held in the Rattan Grounds, FLESSELLES at 10 am. A Canteen number of N.C.O's and men of the Battalion went in a bus to leave	

WAR DIARY
or
INTELLIGENCE SUMMARY.

Army Form C. 2118.

(Erase heading not required.)

Place	Date	Hour	Summary of Events and Information	Remarks and references to Appendices
	1916 Sunday 23rd Jany.		To AMIENS. In the afternoon the Commanding Officer attended a conference with C.R.E. 51st Division at MIRICOURT Chateau when they discussed ways and means of training the Battalion as Pioneers. The day was bright and cold in the morning, but in the afternoon a thick fog settled down.	
	Monday 24th Jany		C and D Companies marched to MONTON VILLERS and continued hut-making, while A and B Companies worked on the "Show ground" trenches. The weather was wet and miserable.	H.Q.
	Tuesday 25th Jany		A & B Companies were engaged on work at MONTON VILLERS making huts, and C and D Companies worked on the Show ground trenches, and C.R.E. held a conference between G.O.C. Division and C.R.E. The idea seems to be to make a complete specimen of trenches showing various kinds	

Army Form C. 2118.

WAR DIARY
or
INTELLIGENCE SUMMARY.

(Erase heading not required.)

Instructions regarding War Diaries and Intelligence
Summaries are contained in F. S. Regs., Part II.
and the Staff Manual respectively. Title pages
will be prepared in manuscript.

Place	Date	Hour	Summary of Events and Information	Remarks and references to Appendices
	Tuesday 25th Jany 9/16		If trench, different patterns, different forms of revetments and bomb stops. They were evidently going to be used for instructing troops freshly arrived in the country – showing them what to avoid. In the evening the commanding officer and other four officers attended a lecture at Lignacourt, 13th Corps Headquarters on the Battle of Loos. The day was cold and fine	H.Q.
	Wednesday 26th Jany.		C and D Companies were again at work hed. making at MONTON VILLERS while A + B Companies were on the show ground trenches. The afternoon was observed as a holiday and a number of officers, NBO's and men were granted leave to AMIENS. The evening was fine + unsettled	H.Q.

2353 Wt. W2544/1454 700,000 5/15 D.D.& L. A.D.S.S./Forms/C. 2118.

WAR DIARY
or
INTELLIGENCE SUMMARY.

(Erase heading not required.)

Army Form C. 2118.

Place	Date	Hour	Summary of Events and Information	Remarks and references to Appendices
	1916			
	Thursday 27th Jany		A and B Companies went over to MONTONVILLERS to continue working at hut-making. C & D Companies were again to Showground trenches. The weather was cold and fair.	S.G.
	Friday 28th Jany.		The Battalion supplied a working party of 1 officer and 125 men to work on the trenches of the Divisional Grenade School. Grand from 9am to 11am & to the afternoon. 4 Grenadier Parties from the Battalion went to the Grenade School to carry out an actual in conjunction with the pupils at the School. The usual parties proceeded to MONTONVILLERS for hut-making and the remainder of the Battalion worked on the Showground trenches. The weather was fair & dry.	S.G.
	Saturday 29th Jany.		The usual working party was again at work at hut-making at MONTONVILLERS. The remainder of the Battalion worked to Showground trenches. The weather was damp and muddy.	S.G.

WAR DIARY
INTELLIGENCE SUMMARY.
(Erase heading not required.)

Army Form C. 2118.

Place	Date 1916	Hour	Summary of Events and Information	Remarks and references to Appendices
	Sunday 30th Jany		Church Parade was held this morning at 10 a.m. in the Chateau Grounds, FLEGSELLES. In the afternoon the team of the Battalion played a football match against the 1/5 Royal Scots but were unfortunately defeated. The weather was extremely cold and misty.	
	Monday 31st Jany		The Battalion completed the work allotted to them in the village of MONTONVILLERS. Work on the "Slow Funnel" trenches was continued, and the officers and men were instructed in sham, cabling, revetment, handling, fascine &c. The day was clear and cold.	

CONFIDENTIAL.

WAR DIARY

of

6th Battalion The Cameronians (Scottish Rifles).

from 1st February 1916 to 29th February 1916.

Vol VIII

left 154 Bde for 33rd Div
2/2/16.

Army Form C. 2118.

WAR DIARY
or
INTELLIGENCE SUMMARY. 1/6th Bn. The Cameronians
(Erase heading not required.)

Instructions regarding War Diaries and Intelligence Summaries are contained in F. S. Regs., Part II. and the Staff Manual respectively. Title pages will be prepared in manuscript.

Place	Date	Hour	Summary of Events and Information	Remarks and references to Appendices
	Tuesday 1st Feby 1916		The whole Battalion were at work on the Slow Round Tracks and received instruction in various forms of Military Engineering. A detachment of 2 Officers and 100 N.C.Os and men left for work at FLESSELLES station under special instructions. 3rd Army men attached to the Battalion for return and described. Lieut Russell R.E. delivered a lecture to all officers on the "Siting of Trenches and Field Fortifications". The day was cold but very fine.	J.T.G. 19 sheets 11 P
	Wednesday 2nd Feby		Companies carried out a route march of about 9 miles in full marching order. Route was TALMAS – VILLERS BOCAGE – FLESSELLES – NAOURS – TALMAS – VILLERS BOCAGE – FLESSELLES. The Companies marched off the afternoon as a holiday. The afternoon was fine but very cold.	J.T.G.
	Thursday 3rd Feby		The whole Battalion were at work on the "Slow Round" Trenches both morning and afternoon. The Lewis Machine Gun Section carried	

2353 Wt. W3411/1454 700,000 5/15 D.D.&L. A.D.S.S./Forms/C. 2118.

WAR DIARY
or
INTELLIGENCE SUMMARY

Army Form C. 2118.

Place	Date	Hour	Summary of Events and Information	Remarks and references to Appendices
Thursday	1916 3rd Feby		out firing practise under the Machine Gun Officer, to signalling Section and at station work and to Stretcher bearers parades under the Medical Officer. the weather was beautiful but exceedingly cold.	
Friday	4th Feby		The Battalion was again at work as on the "Show Ground" Reveille both morning and afternoon. Major Graham motored in to DAOURS to arrange billets for the ——— Battalion. He reported that accommodation was good as to 10 * hops ammunition Reserve Park had been for y 200/70 and had spread themselves over the village. Every twenty soldiers had a hut to himself. So private billets to close them up and but and made Battalion. The day was wet and unsettled.	LL9
Saturday	5th Feby		The Companies carried out a Route march of about 12 miles. Order of march — A.B.C.D. Starting Point — FLESSELLES Route — FLESSELLES — ST VAST — VAUX-en-AMIÉNOIS — FLESSELLES	

WAR DIARY or INTELLIGENCE SUMMARY

Army Form C. 2118.

Place	Date	Hour	Summary of Events and Information	Remarks and references to Appendices
Saturday	5th Feby 1916		**CAPES** Sheet AMIENS 17 Scale 1:100,000. The Commanding Officer and Adjutant rode round and met Companies on the march. The afternoon was spent in bathing and washing, as the men were badly in need of both. Sinks were retimed trench for the purpose and water heated for the men. Says Stones. The process is a slow one as the only water available under the circumstances. 2/Lieut J.W. Hurchess went to Chateau Bylam D Argen Grey appointed Assistant Adjutant to the Battalion by Authority of III Army Commander notified from 16th January 1916. The day was fine and clear.	
Sunday	6th Feby		**Church Parade** was held at 10 a.m. in Chateau Grounds. **FLESSELLES.** The Commanding Officer told Junior Subalterns of Battalion to tell men that they to intended Sylvester's tea and that if they had any suggestions they had up	

Army Form C. 2118.

WAR DIARY
or
INTELLIGENCE SUMMARY.
(Erase heading not required.)

Place	Date	Hour	Summary of Events and Information	Remarks and references to Appendices
	Sunday 6th Feby. 1916		Made then to the Adjutant. The Adjutant afterwards received written objections from the five officers in question who had thoroughly concurred, and replied to them in strongly worded terms. 23 NCOs and men reported sick from the Base at ETAPLES the day was dull and uncertain.	A.G.
	Monday 7th Feby.		The day was spent cleaning up billets and preparing for the move. The commanding officer inspected the billets of all five companies informally in the course of the day. The subalterns referred to in yesterdays entry replied in slightly insubordinate terms to the Adjutant. The recruits for such supervision which had not present staff in the Regular Army in peace time, too awaiting for all branches of the Service serving in the field, one has on par, fortunately to recruits caused efficiency. The morning dawned was wet but after noon it cleared and the weather was fresh and dry.	H.Q.

WAR DIARY or INTELLIGENCE SUMMARY

Army Form C. 2118.

Place	Date	Hour	Summary of Events and Information	Remarks and references to Appendices
Tuesday	8th Feby		The Battalion moved into a new billeting area in DAOURS. Route was through VILLERS-BOCAGE — MOLLIENS au BOIS — ST. GRATIEN — QUERRIEU — DAOURS. (Reference AMIENS SHEET 12 Scale 1:80,000) The Battalion moved at 9am in the following order:- B.C, D. A, Machine Gun Section, Regimental Police and Field Punishment men, and transport. The Battalion was held up for a considerable time on the road as they met the 3rd Division on the march. They arrived in DAOURS about 3pm. The NCOs were billeted in a large mill, 2 companies in each floor. The officers' billets were scattered. The morning was very wet but any scattered about 9am and the remainder of the day was dry and clear.	
Wednesday	9th Feby		The day was spent in cleaning and arranging the new billets and in inspecting the men's feet. The Commanding Officer had	

WAR DIARY or INTELLIGENCE SUMMARY

Army Form C. 2118.

(Erase heading not required.)

Place	Date	Hour	Summary of Events and Information	Remarks and references to Appendices
	Wednesday 9th Feby /1916		all the men who fell out to the march up before him and emphasised to Coy Commanders the necessity of keeping more attention to the men's feet. & the morning snow fell, but the remainder of the day was fine.	
	Thursday 10th Feby		C & D Companies went engaged making new trenches for the Division of General School. ½ mile S.W. of DAOURS. The other two Companies & "B" Paraded at close order drill & so. 2/Lieut W. SIM. joined from 3/6th See Rifles and was posted to "A" Coy. A riding school for junior officers was held in the afternoon. The weather was fine.	ICY
	Friday 11th Feby		The weather was very wet and all parades were abandoned.	ICY
	Saturday 12th Feby		The Battalion commenced work on a new railroad from VECQUEMONT to CONTAY (Refce. Amiens Sheet 12 Scale 1:80,000) This railway is being constructed to relieve the	

WAR DIARY
or
INTELLIGENCE SUMMARY.
(Erase heading not required.)

Army Form C. 2118.

Place	Date	Hour	Summary of Events and Information	Remarks and references to Appendices
Saturday	12th Feby 1916		Traffic to the Mam Line to OR 110 to Railway to MERICOURT and is under the supervision of completed by the 151 No RE. This railway has to be entirely new ground. The station now made new detailed for reconstructing under the Divisional Royal Engineers. The day was unsettled.	JG
Sunday	13th Feby		The Battalion was engaged on the railway tree more from 7.30 am to 12 noon, and the remaining party were at work on the woodcutting under the Divl. R.E. A party of 2 officers and 38 men arrived from the 3/6th Scottish Rifles and 5 NCOs and men from the Base who had been sent thro' sick. He chafed in charge of the regd. They were inspected by the to RD and examined by the Medical Officer. The afternoon was observed as a holiday. The day was unsettled.	JG

WAR DIARY or INTELLIGENCE SUMMARY

Army Form C. 2118.

Place	Date	Hour	Summary of Events and Information	Remarks and references to Appendices
	Monday 14th Feby. 1916		The whole Battalion paraded as strong as possible for work on the Railway, and the same party was again engaged in excavating under the Royal Engineers. Majors of Royal arrived back from Shot Know to Scotland. The Commanding Officer had an interview with G.S.O.1. and C.O. of the 1/8 Royal Scots with reference to the pioneer training of the Battalion and it was decided to discontinue work on the railway in order and to train the men in expiring by day & by night. The day was unsettled and cold	
	Tuesday 15th Feby.		A Regimental School of Instruction under Major A.G. Graham and 3 Sergeant Instructors commenced yesterday. This school is for the purpose of training junior officers and junior	

Place	Date	Hour	Summary of Events and Information	Remarks and references to Appendices
	1916 Tuesday 15th Feby.		N.C.Os in charge words of command, guard mounting, bayonet-fighting etc. The Battalion paraded for route order drill from 9am to 12 noon and in the afternoon under 1/6 /8 Royal Scots for instruction in running. 9 a.m. the evening to parts of 1 officer, 1 N.C.O and 29 men paraded again for instruction in running by day and night. The morning was murky and the day and the weather broke down after noon and turned rain fell.	S.J.
	Wednesday 16th Feby		The Divisional Baths were allotted to the — Battalion today, and the companies bathed in the following order commencing at 9-30 am A, B, C and D. The Companies were also engaged in running under the 1/8 Royal Scots. The men and learning extremely expert at this work. The afternoon was observed as a holiday. The day was wet and unsettled.	S.J.

Army Form C. 2118.

WAR DIARY
or
INTELLIGENCE SUMMARY.
(Erase heading not required.)

Instructions regarding War Diaries and Intelligence Summaries are contained in F.S. Regs., Part II. and the Staff Manual respectively. Title pages will be prepared in manuscript.

Place	Date	Hour	Summary of Events and Information	Remarks and references to Appendices
	Thursday 17th	Feby.	Two Companies were engaged in musketry from 9am till 12 noon while the two Companies paraded for close-order drill for the same period. In the afternoon they changed over. In the evening each Company sent 1 Officer, 1 NCO and 26 men to practise in evening &c. night. The day was dry and misty. D/9	
	Friday 18th	Feby.	The weather was so very wet and inclement that any outdoor training was out of the question. The Companies practised musketry and table télémètre drill in billets D/9	
	Saturday 19th	Feby.	The battalion was again at work on the railway at VECQUEMONT from 7.30 am till 4 pm. Information to-day received that the ——— is n'a allotment of Territorial Force Battalions in France. The 33rd Division, 1st Army to join the Battalion to arrive the 21st instant. The Divisional in the Evening of the ———	

2353 Wt. W2544/1454 700,000 5/15 D.D.&L. A.D.S.S./Forms/C. 2118.

WAR DIARY
or
INTELLIGENCE SUMMARY.

Army Form C. 2118.

Place	Date 1916	Hour	Summary of Events and Information	Remarks and references to Appendices
	Saturday 19th Feby		The resting Transport Officer with men to MERICOURT to make necessary arrangements for entrainment. The day was wet and unsettled.	
	Sunday 20th Feby.		The Battalion was again engaged working on the railway at VECQUEMONT from 7.30 am to 3 pm. 25 N.C.Os and men as reinforcements arrived from the Base Depot. 15 of these were from 3/6 W. Yorks. Rifles and the rest. Ten men were exchanged for horse-shoers at night. The enemy made an air-raid on AMIENS about 10-15 pm. The sound of the explosion of the bombs could be heard distinctly. The day was fine.	
	Monday 21st Feby.		The Battalion entrained at MERICOURT at 11pm to proceed to join the 33rd Division, 1st Army, after a	

WAR DIARY or INTELLIGENCE SUMMARY

Army Form C. 2118.

Place	Date	Hour	Summary of Events and Information	Remarks and references to Appendices
Monday	21st Feb 1916		From journey of 9 hours, arrived at a station near ANNEZIN about 2-15am. The Battalion detrained and marched to BETHUNE. Before leaving, the G.O.C. 51st Division and the G.S.O.1. came to say good-bye to the Battalion, and altogether the Division gave us an splendid send-off. The day and the night especially were very cold and wearied. When the Battalion arrived in ANNEZIN, the Colonel and several Officers and invited men and its adjutant to Headquarters. The Battalion is billeted at Division of Reinforcement in the 100th Bgd. The 15th being the 1/7 Middlesex Battalion and 1 seems a splendid Pioneer Battalion.	
Tuesday	22nd Feb		There was a shower Battalion and netherlands next of a splendid Pioneer Battalion	SAAT 9/16

WAR DIARY or INTELLIGENCE SUMMARY

Place	Date	Hour	Summary of Events and Information	Remarks and references to Appendices
	Tuesday 22nd July 1916		The day was devoted to Lewis Rifle, especially as we have spent such a long time training as Pioneers. Ranks were consequently thin, reflecting hours of training the Lewis Gun Section and Bombing. There was a very heavy fall of snow during the day accompanied by extreme cold.	SF9
	Wednesday 23rd Sept.		The morning was spent in cleaning up billets and mustering kit equipment &c, and in afternoon was observed as a holiday. The Commanding Officer Lieutenant Colonel Airerd commanding 10th Brigade and discussed matters common to the Battalion. So there was a heavy fall of snow during the day and to-night the snow was very low.	SF9

WAR DIARY
INTELLIGENCE SUMMARY

Army Form C. 2118.

Place	Date	Hour	Summary of Events and Information	Remarks and references to Appendices
	Thursday 24th Feby		The Brigade paraded the morning from 9-10am to Noon for Close order drill etc and also for inspection of kits Blankets S.A.A, iron rations and rifles covers. The Lewis Gun officer reported at Brigade Headquarters at 9am and received instructions the time with Bde H. Qs. to receive instructions that he was to go in to the lines tomorrow with his 4 guns. The Bn was less and front by the Battalion moved into a new billeting area this afternoon in ANNEQUIN NORTH.	
	Friday 25th Feby		Brigade Route: ANNEQUIN — BETHUNE — BEUVRY — ANNEQUIN NORTH. Time: 9am. Starting point: Battn Orderly Room. The Transport Officer moved off with the Transport to BEUVRY to take over the horse standings of 16th Middx to Quarter and Stores Guards at BEUVRY, and the Quartermaster

WAR DIARY or INTELLIGENCE SUMMARY

Army Form C. 2118.

Place	Date	Hour	Summary of Events and Information	Remarks and references to Appendices
Friday	10/6 23/4/15	Day	Also took over a Battalion Store in BETHUNE. The Battalion relieved the 2nd Worcesters in support Reserve and furnished working parties for the trenches. Every available man required for this and so the Battalion is much under strength, it does seem hard on the men, the Brigade Division as very few new drafts arrived and the B[attalion] was in the trenches and very few rest. The Battn was in Division for six days before any sufficient rest was received. The discipline and saluting of all arms of service in Hinderland and the new army units is appalling and subject to C.O. France a report to 3rd Bde H.Qrs on subject. A general air of slackness and inefficiency is very noticeable in all ranks the day was bitterly cold and there was a heavy fall of snow	

Place	Date	Hour	Summary of Events and Information	Remarks and references to Appendices
	1916			
Trenches	Saturday 26th		The Battalion were relieved of funnel working parties this date except men in the Battalion. Working parties and day in relays. The commanding officer held a conference of Coy Commanders in the morning and in the afternoon the Coy Commanders went up to the line to inspect it. The day was not so cold as previously and no further snow fell.	
	Sunday 27th		The Battalion received orders to relieve the 2nd Worcesters in the Trenches in A.2 Sub in the evening of the 28th instant. All Company Commanders, Lewis Gun officers and Sniper officers went to the line and to Coy HQrs of 2nd Worcesters to make the necessary arrangements for the relief. Owing to a conference of Coy Commanders being held and all the arrangements attached to this, Commanders was considered difficult for relieving of a Bn so weak in numbers.	

Place	Date	Hour	Summary of Events and Information	Remarks and references to Appendices
	Sunday 27th Feb		It was arranged however for the Battalion to be relieved by the 7th K.R.R. & the rest of the B.G. to remain in trenches. The day was cold but dry.	
	Monday 28th Feb		The relief was completed in good time at 2.15 pm and the Adjutant went up at 6 pm. The Companies commenced at 6.30 pm for the station of communication then in 1/2 hours. Following orders D. & A C. at 1/2 Coy interval. B Coy relieved the reserve Company at 6 am in the morning to enable the 2nd Worcester to relieve us from the permanent working parties provided by the Battalion in trenches. During the section of Armenius trenches was that O'Leary won his V.C.	

WAR DIARY or INTELLIGENCE SUMMARY

Army Form C. 2118.

Place	Date	Hour	Summary of Events and Information	Remarks and references to Appendices
	19/10 Tuesday 19th Oct		The day was quiet in trenches. Nothing of any note occurring. Colonel Chaplin Comdg 1st Cameronians came to mess to CO preparatory to relieving the Bath the next day. Bay. Commanders attended a conference and all arrangements for the relief were made. The clerical work entailed in the Division on account of an advance is enormous & returns of all means of the British Army. A Battalion spend all the time answering queries by the Staff or readdresses & issue of orders due to countermanding of orders. The day was fine.	

ATTACHED.
33RD DIVISION
100TH INFY BDE

51 DIVISION
154 BDE

6TH BN SCOTTISH RIFLES
(CAMERONIANS)
MAR - MAY 1916

WAR DIARY
or
INTELLIGENCE SUMMARY

Army Form C. 2118.

6th B. The Camerons (Scottish Rifles)

10/3

Mar '16 / May '16

Place	Date	Hour	Summary of Events and Information	Remarks and references to Appendices
[Béthune]	Wednesday 31st March 1916		The Battalion was relieved in the trenches by the 10th Gordons. The Gordons Bombers and Snipers as well as the Lewis Gun section relieved during the day. The relief commenced about 5.30pm and was completed about 9.30pm the position of Companies being responsible for the relief being the same as their 2 excursions into the trenches. The relief of the Battalion forces into LE QUESNOY at 8. 8.42 (Refer BETHUNE Sheet). The day was fine.	Mar '16 / May '16
	Thursday 20th March		The day was spent cleaning up kit, equipment and little inspections of feet, arms and rifles were held. The day was cold and wet.	29

WAR DIARY
or
INTELLIGENCE SUMMARY

(Erase heading not required.)

Army Form C. 2118.

Place	Date	Hour	Summary of Events and Information	Remarks and references to Appendices
	Friday 5th March		The Battalion and Regiment marched were inspected by Major General d.G.S. Carter G.O.C. 33rd Division at 11 am. He was accompanied by his A.A.Q.M.G. and the Brigadier 100th Inf. Bde. Bde. He seemed quite pleased with general appearance of Battalion. The day was dull but dry.	
	Saturday 6th March		The Battalion were allotted to baths at BEUVRY, but as usual every of no use to Staff arrangements, they were Bath Other than did not expect anyone in consequence had no clean shirts nearly a list of recommendations for honours forwards were asked for and were forwards There was a heavy fall of snow during the day.	

WAR DIARY or INTELLIGENCE SUMMARY

Army Form C. 2118.

Place	Date	Hour	Summary of Events and Information	Remarks and references to Appendices
	Sunday 5th March 1916		Church Parade was held at BEUVRY at 11am. The service was conducted by a communion service to the 5th Scots Rifles. The afternoon was observed as a holiday. The day was fine but unsettled.	
	Monday 6th March		The Battalion were allotted to Baths and tombonies availed themselves of chance of being set of cess. and then they received in exchange from the other units to Anel, the run was spent in suitable place cleaning of billets	
	Tuesday 7th March		115 Officers and men marched to ESSARS to witness a demonstration to public of Gen. an. Hammenwerfer. The demonstration was	

WAR DIARY or INTELLIGENCE SUMMARY

Place	Date 1916	Hour	Summary of Events and Information	Remarks and references to Appendices
	Tuesday 4th April		conducted by the Technical Adviser with the T.M. Army and proved conclusively to those present that this form of frightfulness was terrifying but really harmless. The afternoon was given to meeting agents, improving abodes accomodation.	
	Wednesday 5th April		Creating brick pathways to the huts. Revue Battalion moved into the Brigade tactical command of ANNEQUIN SOUTH and came under to the O.C. 99 Inf. Bgde relief the Brigades were complete Route: LEQUESNOY - BEUVRY - LA BASSEE ROAD - ANNEQUIN SOUTH. T M's 12.45 p.m. Order of hand ADC and MO Seaton B Echelon while in Brigade Reserve must always be ready to turn out on a half hours notice the day was	S.S.9

WAR DIARY
or
INTELLIGENCE SUMMARY.

(Erase heading not required.)

Army Form C. 2118.

Place	Date	Hour	Summary of Events and Information	Remarks and references to Appendices
	Wednesday 9th March 1916		The Battalion supplied working parties to the trenches as per usual. These men who were left were engaged in cleaning up and repairing the Grenadier parade under the Bath Sheds. Officers as usual. There was a heavy bombardment by our Artillery on the enemy's line efforts where an attempt was kept up but an attack was not attempted there. The weather was good. Snow but otherwise	DG 89
	Thursday 16th March		The Battalion still continues to be working. Parties to the tunnelling Company. to pun a drive to A.D.M.S. parades under the Batt. Grenadier Officer. and Confinements to the C.O. inspected the hutts. The Officers were issued with their ventilation steel Helmets with orders to wear them always in the forward area and they are all day	DG

WAR DIARY
or
INTELLIGENCE SUMMARY

Army Form C. 2118.

Place	Date	Hour	Summary of Events and Information	Remarks and references to Appendices
	1916 Saturday 11th March		The Battalion supplied the usual working parties to the Tunnelling Coy. Captain & that returned from the Base Hospital and took over command of A Coy. Captain D.J. Colwill joined the Battalion from Scotland and was posted to A Coy as second in command. Captain J Ham was transferred to B Coy as second in command. H. Coy. H.Q. was in Rain.	
	Sunday 12th March		The commanding officer went to a conference at Brigade H.Q.s. Major Boyd and Coy Commanders went to the adjutant and A Coy to the trenches when Z.1 sub section of Trots was taken over from Battalion. There was a conference of Coy. Commanders in the afternoon to discuss the synopsis. The weather was beautiful and upon H.Q. final arrangements were made.	

Army Form C. 2118.

WAR DIARY
or
INTELLIGENCE SUMMARY.
(Erase heading not required.)

Instructions regarding War Diaries and Intelligence Summaries are contained in F.S. Regs., Part II. and the Staff Manual respectively. Title pages will be prepared in manuscript.

Place	Date	Hour	Summary of Events and Information	Remarks and references to Appendices
	1916 Monday 13th March		The Battalion relieved the 2nd Worcesters in AUCHY Sector for Boyanses 1 to 8 (Refs. Trench Map 36c. N.W.¹) The relief commenced about 5-30pm and was completed about 8-45pm. The trenches & dugouts after to be good. In this part of the line between our trenches and those of the enemy is very flat and the wire is not very good on our side. General Gordon visited the trenches in the morning and had a few very minor complaints to make. The various officers & men who had been on courses returned to duty the day & the weather splendid and very warm.	
	Tuesday 14th March		This morning the enemy blew up a mine about 120 yards from no man's land and immediately	

WAR DIARY
or
INTELLIGENCE SUMMARY

Army Form C. 2118.

Place	Date	Hour	Summary of Events and Information	Remarks and references to Appendices
	Tuesday 16 March		Threats replied it was afterwards attributed to A 29 & B.2 about 60 yards out. Sgt. Shiel ran out from Bryan & Clegue, head shot 36 C. N.W. Edition (?) They had evidently carefully prepared a scheme of plantation and there were two salvos of shell two for the skies about 7 am. to artillery with rifle grenades killed 22 minutes later into the German reserve trenches who managed to get to afternoon. They fired turned on it to kills with good effect. A combined about "Staff" was arranged with rifle grenades and 15 pounders.	

WAR DIARY
or
INTELLIGENCE SUMMARY.

Army Form C. 2118.

Place	Date	Hour	Summary of Events and Information	Remarks and references to Appendices
	Sunday 14th March 1915		Commencing in the evening at 11 pm and continuing at intervals till 10 am. to next morning the Germans worked hard to consolidate their position but due to the nature of ground ad to together further to-operation very little could be done to prevent them. We suffered some casualties to about 1 officer & 3 other ranks wounded to say nothing of	929
Wednesday 17th March			The day was quiet on the whole the enemy fired a large number of rifle grenades into our ad we retaliated strongly with rifle grenades. The day saw Bn. 9th recover	929

WAR DIARY
or
INTELLIGENCE SUMMARY.

Army Form C. 2118.

(Erase heading not required.)

Place	Date	Hour	Summary of Events and Information	Remarks and references to Appendices
	Thursday 16th Nov.		The enemy were again active with rifle grenade and trench Guns. We sustained several casualties. 2 killed and wounded. Several officers of the non-survivors visited the line with a view to taking it over. They were shown round the line by us. To 6.0. There – nothing of an important nature was shown on 18 Pdr or Vickers or Battery (same place) Guns. 29.0 H.E. (?) very about Left of Sect.	
	Friday 17th Nov.		From rifle grenades fell in our lines and no further casualties. Three officers of the new division came to the trenches to be shown to the line 2.0 to 3.0 — 2nd Worcesters. We were relieved by	

WAR DIARY
or
INTELLIGENCE SUMMARY.

Place	Date	Hour	Summary of Events and Information	Remarks and references to Appendices
Friday 14th March	1916		attack about 9am. and proceeded to billets in ANNEQUIN SOUTH as Battalion in Brigade Reserve. We took over the remainder working day to France at 5 p.m. and consequently 3 Platoons in the afternoon. We were relieved by the 750 yards long with 260 like a line of men of when 60 were in support reserve. We are new excepting the Worcesters who worked in consequence that strength are more than double the at of told the some of his eight the enemy attacked two of the craters	29
Saturday 15th March			on HOHENZOLLERN REDOUBT and its short barrage tell all round the village of	

WAR DIARY or INTELLIGENCE SUMMARY

Army Form C. 2118.

Place	Date	Hour	Summary of Events and Information	Remarks and references to Appendices
ANNEQUIN SOUTH	Saturday 18th March 1916		We suffered about 8 casualties and latterly received orders from Brigade to send a Company up to AUCHY Sector — right support. They were not required and returned in the morning. The Revd. gent Bryan Swain SCF was killed.	
	Sunday 19th		Supports by returned Hollis at 3am been w/c to RAILWAY KEEP. Deflund Church Parade at 11am by the new Padre Rev. Mr Beveridge. Went parties as usual. Day bright and warm.	
	Monday 20th March		The adjutant Ourford fired into influenza. One man notably injured by Cherry D. Ank - air craft still fell in him. He died after our after. With parties as usual. Saw received instruction that the Battalion was to relieve the 2nd Worcester Tomorrow. Lieut D. Cox Campbell. ADSS. Wd. at 2 p.m. and the Adjt. sent w/o to	

WAR DIARY
or
INTELLIGENCE SUMMARY

Army Form C. 2118.

Place	Date	Hour	Summary of Events and Information	Remarks and references to Appendices
Monden	20 March		Anzac details & others Colonel Kerr received instructions from the Brigadier to keep one Company Stoke and Worcester in the Trenches & act in reserve. Owing to our weak condition. Day warm & dull	
Tuesday	21 March		Work parties in morning. "D" Company (D"Coy (C/K.I.) 5)th Worcester in E daytime. Relief complete at 8/10 p.m. Line was to be manned by Worcesters Take over our 6 p.m. work parties. The remainder of the battalion left CAMBRIN CHURCH at 5 p.m. in the relief was complete at 8.30 p.m. The night order is A, B, C, D fit & in other ranks.	NPMe
Wednesday	22 March		Enemy very quiet last night. Few rifle grenades were more than usually wounded. No artillery activity to speak of on either side throughout the day, the enemy were very quiet. Our grenadiers fired a few rifle grenades in the morning. In even- ing pre-arrangement a raid was carried out by the 1st Queen's on our left. We co-operated with the German trenches in the vicinity of MINE POINT. rifle & machine gun fire, a special force of grenadiers from the 16th K.R.R. fired rifle grenades from HIGH ST. Raid commenced at 8.22 and ended about 8.40. No casualties except a slight wound to one of the Queen's officers. Day was dull & wet	
Thursday	23 March		Night except for above was very quiet. Very dark. Sent one platoon of "A" Coy. Company on a patrol. Went out from "A" Coy. at 11/0 p.m. & found the enemy working	

WAR DIARY
or
INTELLIGENCE SUMMARY

Army Form C. 2118.

Place	Date	Hour	Summary of Events and Information	Remarks and references to Appendices
	Thursday March 23		In MADAGASCAR Trench just to north of new crater. No work actually been done in scarly itself. Colonel DOUGLAS 5/KSR arrived & made arrangements about relieving us tomorrow night. At 3.30 pm four Company Commanders, Intelligence Officer, bombing officer and M.G.O. from 5/KSR arrived at Bn H.Q. to view line. After about an hour bombardment the enemy exploded a small mine near our front & opposite lines held by 1st QUEENS. Test fired gas alarm carried out by Baynage at 10.30 a.m. Battalion was "standing to" at 10.40 p.m. when ordered when from to "stand down". Special helmets were drawn for this occasion from Major J. Can. Commander.	
	Friday March 24		Very quiet night with slight rain shower in morning. Relief of Coy commanders at 10.30 a.m. Major BOYD with 1 NCO & 1 man each Company left for ANNAZIN at 10 pm for billets temporaire. Battalion was relieved by 5th Leo Rifles about 10-30 pm and marched to ANNEZIN in a downpour of snow & sleet. They arrived here about 2 am. The same had arrangements about the relief and the snow in general were again noticeable. The day was very wet & a great deal of snow fell.	

WAR DIARY
or
INTELLIGENCE SUMMARY.

Army Form C. 2118.

Place	Date	Hour	Summary of Events and Information	Remarks and references to Appendices
	Saturday 25th March 1916		The day was spent cleaning up billets and clothes and equipment. The Rev. W.W. Seaver C.F. Chaplain to the Forces joined the Battalion for duty vice the 9th Royal Scots. The day was fine and dry.	S.D.
	Sunday 26th March		Church Parade was held in the Ecurie Sheds ANNEZIN at 11 am. The remainder of the day was observed as a holiday. The weather was mild but dry.	S.D.
	Monday 27th March		Various courses in Bombing, Lewis Gun, Signalling & commenced to-day under Brigade arrangements. The rates at BETHUNE were allotted to the Battalion and to Companies. Battle training morning and afternoon the Coys Commanders. Held a conference of all officers of the 100th Bn of Coys to the purpose of training for their attack. XVI Corps Commander B. Gen Sir Richard Haking K.C.B.	

Army Form C. 2118.

WAR DIARY
or
INTELLIGENCE SUMMARY.
(Erase heading not required.)

Instructions regarding War Diaries and Intelligence Summaries are contained in F. S. Regs., Part II. and the Staff Manual respectively. Title pages will be prepared in manuscript.

Place	Date	Hour	Summary of Events and Information	Remarks and references to Appendices
	1916			
	Monday 27th		Commanding Officer rode with to Corps H.Q.Ques. Commander in chief, on to Ey Bde. to R.Q. Sent in a letter to Brigade stating in case of Battalion meet regard to shortage of numbers and saying that at present we could Battalion. Other any grumbittes was rest and the day was spent	
	Tuesday 28th		Companies carried out route marches under Company arrangements and set to Headquarters staff rode round and means companies on to march. The day was butterby cold with a strong wind	
	Wednesday 29th		Companies paraded for close order drill, Physical exercises and musketry in the morning and in the afternoon in the afternoon engaged in firing and a Box Car platoon. The day was fine	

WAR DIARY
INTELLIGENCE SUMMARY.

(Erase heading not required.)

Place	Date	Hour	Summary of Events and Information	Remarks and references to Appendices
Thursday	1916 30th March		The Companies carried out a training in supplying Working Parties. Battalion has used up to second line defences which consisted in wiring the Battalion Lewis Gun near LE PREOL and BEUVRY. School paraded as usual under the M.G.O. and the Grenadier School under the Grenadier Officer. LG — was fine and bright.	
Friday	31st March		The Brigadier General ordered to Brigade inspected the transport section and seemed quite satisfied with the condition of men also vehicles. The A.S.M.S. inspected the billets and gave orders to the Battalion had to supply fate gue parties to clear away civilian refuse which was considerable. The Companies paraded for close order drill & a C.O. Company [?] Football match in the afternoon. The day was beautiful and even LG used indulged	

WAR DIARY
or
INTELLIGENCE SUMMARY. 6th Bn. The Cameronians

Army Form C.-2118.

Place	Date 1916	Hour	Summary of Events and Information	Remarks and references to Appendices
	Saturday 1st April		Boys carried out a route march under Company arrangements. A fatigue party was at work clearing up rubbish and heaps of several tons in attempts to remove signs of Service months. The Battalion's Reported to M/so Field Ambulance at period and cleared them.	
	Sunday 2nd April		Church Parade was held at Ham in the Cinema House, ANNEZIN. The work of clearing up and disposing of the accumulation of rubbish and refuse was carried out. In the afternoon the Battalion moved to a new billeting area in LE QUESNOY at 3-30 pm via BETHUNE – LA BASSEE RD – BEUVRY – LE QUESNOY – billets there at 5 pm and Bat. was relieved from the 16 K.R.R. The billets here is a little to ditto. The day was beautiful and bright & continued to have to Scotland warm	

WAR DIARY or INTELLIGENCE SUMMARY

Army Form C. 2118.

Place	Date 1916	Hour	Summary of Events and Information	Remarks and references to Appendices
Monday	3rd April		Hand went 20 parades to day. The time was spent on cleaning up the rifles and ground. Something commenced. A Batt. Bayonet fighting school was commenced, and gallows erected. This school was in charge of the officer who had returned from the Brigade School. The Battalion Lewis Gun School and Grenadier School were again in operation and at rest. Weather was attended that day and very warm.	
Tuesday	4th April		The C.O., Adjutant and Coy Commanders went up to the trenches in "Auchy" Right with a view to making arrangements for taking over the Battalion. The following day the Battalion was a service Battalion, the 16th P.P.B. who were in the line for instruction. The day was any but	

WAR DIARY
or
INTELLIGENCE SUMMARY.
(Erase heading not required.)

Army Form C. 2118.

Place	Date	Hour	Summary of Events and Information	Remarks and references to Appendices
	Wednesday 5th April 1916		The men had 10 parades in the morning, to the Lewis Guns in cleaning of billets and disposing of refuse and rubbish. The Battalion relieved the 16th Rifle Brigade in the trenches in CUINCHY RIGHT. They were augmented by 2 Companies of the 2nd Worcesters. Reliefs they were so much. The relief commenced at 6-45 pm and was completed by 8-65. Bombers orders as new relieves as the Bns. of the afternoon. The 16th Rifle Brigade had all the characteristics of a Service Battalion, in other words the men unwilling to learn stunts to rifles to Battalion trenches. 2 casualties (2 men killed). The day was fine and warm 79.	

Army Form C. 2118.

WAR DIARY
or
INTELLIGENCE SUMMARY.
(Erase heading not required.)

Instructions regarding War Diaries and Intelligence Summaries are contained in F.S. Regs., Part II. and the Staff Manual respectively. Title pages will be prepared in manuscript.

Place	Date	Hour	Summary of Events and Information	Remarks and references to Appendices
	1916 Thursday 6th April		The trenches were fairly quiet in the morning, but in the afternoon the enemy sent over a large number of trench mortars & right and trench mortar & bomb and also a considerable amount of damage to several newer trenches. The enemy shelled CUINCHY SUPPORT POINT and BRADDELL CASTLE in course of the afternoon and damaged the wirehead wiring in HERTFORD ST. No men were wounded. The day was fine and warm.	JCG
	Friday 7th April		Two companies of 7th K.R.R.C. 39th Division were attached to the Battalion for instruction and relieved two companies of the 2nd Worcesters who returned to ANNEQUIN NORTH. Six of 7th & 22 went into the front line to after noon. The enemy threw relieving Coys. Bombs and trench mortars again from heavy. Rifle and artillery fire very heavy.	

Place	Date	Hour	Summary of Events and Information	Remarks and references to Appendices
	1916			
Friday	7th April		went reconnoitring. As to artillery were on short ration and so he had no tenth mortars in last line save an old "Acheless", the retaliation was as usual expected to adequate. Retaliation is up any use must be quick and heavy. However to the CRA Bde have promised so a find kind of mortar which will beat anything to Germans had, he can remember listening to the same promises for a year ago for some and line.	
Saturday	8th April		Day zero warm and fine. The Germans were again active with French front. Mortars on our front. Retaliation was asked for when the Hamiltons and others in a small degree. The 2nd Dorsets CO and the Commodore came up to make arrangements for to relief. Regt. the Battalion was relieved in GUINCHY & Right	

WAR DIARY
or
INTELLIGENCE SUMMARY.
(Erase heading not required.)

Army Form C. 2118.

Place	Date	Hour	Summary of Events and Information	Remarks and references to Appendices
	Saturday 8th April 1916		Sector bright. Relief by the 2nd Worcesters Relief commenced at 4pm and was complete by 9pm. the Battalion in relief proceeded to ANNEQUIN NORTH. The day was dull and unsettled.	J.G.
	Sunday 9th April		The Battalion supplied to usual working parties to 35st St Emillio Colliery until 5pm when the reliefs were taken over by the KRR 6 to advance parts of Platoons from the Battalion moved off to ANNEQUIN NORTH, ANNEQUIN SOUTH and ANNEQUIN FOSSE the enemy shelled Battalion rezvd(?) at Fort time. To Battalion reorganised west of BEUVRY and marched into BETHUNE to billets in Ecole des Jeunes Filles, Rue 5th Batt. were billeted there also. The day was charming and spring was in the air.	J.G.

Army Form C. 2118.

WAR DIARY
or
INTELLIGENCE SUMMARY.
(Erase heading not required.)

Instructions regarding War Diaries and Intelligence Summaries are contained in F. S. Regs., Part II. and the Staff Manual respectively. Title pages will be prepared in manuscript.

Place	Date	Hour	Summary of Events and Information	Remarks and references to Appendices
	1916			
	Monday 10th April		The day was spent cleaning up equipment and clothing and holding inspection. Kit, feet, &c. &c. 1 O.R. for a run in the 1st Battalion also at L.E.	
QUESNOY	Tuesday 11th April		The day was very bright and warm. Coys paraded for their ordr. drill, musketry, Bayonet fighting &c. from 9 a.m. to 12 noon and again from 2 pm to 4 pm. The day was fair but unsettled.	29
	Wednesday 12th April		The Battalion paraded at 9 a.m. as army not move a about 6 miles. & afternoon was devoted to Football. A working party of 2 officers & 50 men supplied to "JOIN CHY" Regt. Left camp a new trench at 2-15 pm Capt Q.G.H. LOUDON returned from leave to day &c &c.	29

2353 Wt. W25H/1454 700,000 5/15 D. D. & L. A.D.S.S./Form/C. 2118.

WAR DIARY or INTELLIGENCE SUMMARY

Army Form C.2118.

Place	Date	Hour	Summary of Events and Information	Remarks and references to Appendices
Thursday	13th April		The CO and the Adjutant and the Company Commanders went to the trenches in BOINCHY RIGHT to see and to reconnoitre and arrangements for the relief. The two Coys to-aided for close order drill formed up. The Coys had musketry & extended drill from 9am to 12 noon. I the CO Seeing the supplied a working party to the trenches from 5pm to 2-15 am. The day was very wet.	
Friday	14th April		and menths had to more of the totts of East end of the Battalion reflections from 8-30am to 2-30pm. Battalion moved off was held and then had tea on. at 4pm then to trenches as Battalion the reach just outside of BEUVRY to relieved the 1st K.R.R.C in CUINCHY Right. The relief commenced at 7pm and was completed at 9-15pm. The day was very wet and the men	

WAR DIARY or INTELLIGENCE SUMMARY

Army Form C. 2118.

Place	Date	Hour	Summary of Events and Information	Remarks and references to Appendices
Friday	4th April		Things went fairly quiet in the trenches. The Battalion was again augmented by 2 Coys of the 2nd Worcesters. G the enemy at 7-30 p.m. 2 mines were exploded near his lines on the AWHY LEFT Sector. The was followed by a raid by the Infantry which was very successful. We co operated with Trench Mortars, Rifle Grenades and Hills bombs. The enemy was Lift by us Right they fired the SP which to us also but that day.	
Saturday	5th April		Things were again fairly quiet in the trenches, and all sustained no casualties. To Commanding Officer & Second in Command of Scotland. It Company of to Latter Company is off duty from the field hours 10 p.m. Light relieved by the other Company is in Support. A test Gas alarm was tried in front line all anti gas precautions worked smartly and the whole Battalion warning from to alarm was given in 15 minutes after sounding.	

WAR DIARY or INTELLIGENCE SUMMARY

Army Form C. 2118.

Place	Date	Hour	Summary of Events and Information	Remarks and references to Appendices
Salisbury	14th April Saturday		The day was dull and unsettling.	Hy
	15th April Sunday		The enemy was again active with heavy trench mortars on our front. Batteries answered artillery reply. A severe strain for "Curchy Post" subsector was kept up and ready to repair. A report on the Gas alarm was forwarded to the Brigade. The number of clearing Bazar 28 and Short Cut. was proceeded with. The day was fine. Dry and only.	HQ
	16th April Monday		The Officers of the 5th Scottish Rifles came up to the trenches to go round to line preparatory to taking over. All arrangements for the relief were made. Information was received that the 9 1/2 GR 4 & SH had been very successful in g Pass Captured some very important	

WAR DIARY or INTELLIGENCE SUMMARY

Army Form C. 2118.

Place	Date	Hour	Summary of Events and Information	Remarks and references to Appendices
Cuinchy	Monday 19th April		Movements. The day was quiet and was comfortable.	HQ
Cuinchy	Tuesday 20th April		The enemy were again active but although they damaged to our front line fairly, no casualties resulted. The Battalion was relieved by the 1 to 3 K.O. Rifles in "CUINCHY RIGHT". The relief commenced at 7.15 & was completed by 9.15 p.m. On completion of the relief the Battalion marched to BETHUNE on completion of the relief the day via Le Col des Jeunes Filles. The day was quiet and unsettled.	HQ
	Wednesday 21st April		The day was spent in cleaning up and resting. Men and their surroundings and equipment and kits. Little instructions of equipment and clothing. The CO held a meeting of all officers and indulged in a general and comprehensive "shape" the day was not and unsettled	HQ

WAR DIARY or INTELLIGENCE SUMMARY

Army Form C. 2118.

(Erase heading not required.)

Place	Date 1916	Hour	Summary of Events and Information	Remarks and references to Appendices
	Thursday 20th April		The Battalion left the baths in École des Jeunes Filles and the Boys bathed in the old C.D. B.A. and Company Sewing Class. The remainder of the Battalion was devoted to inspection of equipment and the fitting of the D.V.S. 1st Army inspected all its animals. The Battalion. Lt. Col. J.W. Stalin, who was formerly Adjutant of the Battalion and now commands the 13th Royal Sussex visited the Battalion. The day was fair.	
	Friday 21st April		The Boys paraded from 9 am to 12 noon and again from 2pm to 4pm for the usual Boys drill. Coy drill, Battalion Drill. Extended Order Drill, Bayonet fighting. Boys in Attack to Recruits including M.G. Section operated with the Platoon in attack. Ten officers in the morning and ten in the afternoon proceeded to Langlon Corner to Langlon Inspector of Gas and afterwards to view a mine including Close Work and tip laying there. Crater was carefully examined. The Orderly programme for tomorrow	

WAR DIARY or INTELLIGENCE SUMMARY

Army Form C. 2118.

Place	Date 1916	Hour	Summary of Events and Information	Remarks and references to Appendices
	Saturday 22nd April		The streets were very wet and cold and the Brigade route marching was therefore had to be postponed. Lieut Hamptons carried on in shops with musketry and lecture. The Brigadier inspected & Regimental transport.	JG
	Sunday 23rd April		Church Parade was held in the unfinished Chapel in Rue d'Aire at 10 a.m. The remainder of the day was observed as a holiday. The weather was very warm and bright.	JG
	Monday 24th April		The Battalion took part in a Brigade Route March. Route through OBLINGHEM, up towards St. MARQUOIS then thro' GONNEHEM, thence to CHOQUES and back to BETHUNE (Refer BETHUNE combined sheet). The march started at 9am and was finished by 1–30 p.m. Distance about 12 miles. The General did not accompany the Brigade but watched it passing the starting point and at other points on the route. The day was bright and warm. The day was observed as a holiday.	JG

WAR DIARY or INTELLIGENCE SUMMARY

Army Form C. 2118.

Place	Date 1916	Hour	Summary of Events and Information	Remarks and references to Appendices
	Tuesday 25th April		The Coys went for a Short Route March followed by the taking up of a Defence Outpost Scheme, and on the way home they practised Protection while on the move. In the afternoon, they again paraded for extended order drill, field helmet drill and bayonet fighting. In the evening all officers attended a lecture by Lieut Carter and the who had recently returned from a course of instruction at the Divisional School HQ. The day was bright and warm.	
	Wednesday 26th April		The day was spent in cleaning up of billets and in inspection of equipment arms &c. In the afternoon about 6-30 p.m. the Battalion moved into ANNEQUIN SOUTH into available Artillery to relieve the 1st Middlesex. Hand was constructed about activity in the HOHEN ZOLLERN front as we marched ANNEQUIN SOUTH about 8-30 p.m. this routine was well on into the night. The day was bright and very warm. HQ	

W. Deed

WAR DIARY
or
INTELLIGENCE SUMMARY

Army Form C. 2118.

Place	Date	Hour	Summary of Events and Information	Remarks and references to Appendices
016	Thursday 27th April		The enemy shelled ANNEQUIN SOUTH and ANNEQUIN FOSSE with heavy shells from 5 am to 9.30 am. About 6.30 am, a heavy gas cloud passed over our billets and all the Battalion stood to with the hills. Klinets B. the gas had been sent over to the N. Division at Front. South of HOHENZOLLERN on and road turned at right angles & gone north. It was partly strong and some men lost. Int of the Battalion who had not Ken Klinets was passed to several working parties, and the shelter suffered. No employed men improving the shelters not to This day was very heavy & sultry LG east end of village. No Battery at to shelled The enemy again the east as we casualty. We working parties were again Supplies and more none to vicinity of the wood trenches, to	
today	28th April			

WAR DIARY
or
INTELLIGENCE SUMMARY.

(Erase heading not required.)

Army Form C. 2118.

Place	Date	Hour	Summary of Events and Information	Remarks and references to Appendices
	Friday 28th April 1916		The day was bright and very warm	HQ
	Saturday 29th April		The C.O. Adjutant and Coy Commanders visited the trenches on "AUCHY" right preparatory to taking over from the 2nd Worcesters to 30 ft. The line to be taken over by us was shortened to its fast extent severely on its strength is very small in fact severely so. 2/Lieut J.M. DENHOLM appeared in the Gazette as a Lieutenant. The day was very bright & very warm.	HQ
	Sunday 30th April		The Batalion relieved the 2nd Worcesters in the trenches on "Auchy" Right. The relief commenced at 8pm and was complete by 10pm. The weather was very dry and warm.	HQ

XXXIII
(60)

½ AO
33

1/6 Scottish Rifles

Vol XVII

R. P.
18 sheets

Army Form C. 2118.

WAR DIARY
or
INTELLIGENCE SUMMARY.
(Erase heading not required.)

Instructions regarding War Diaries and Intelligence Summaries are contained in F. S. Regs., Part II. and the Staff Manual respectively. Title pages will be prepared in manuscript.

Place	Date	Hour	Summary of Events and Information	Remarks and references to Appendices
	Tuesday 9th May		Various patrols were sent out and a considerable amount of firing was done. The day was fine & very warm	A9
	Wednesday 10 May		The enemy shelled us with heavy stuff to which we replied. Back Street and High Street ad. wells. Casualties 1 man killed and 1 wounded. Sniping continues on all posts. Still active.	
			Raiders on roofs to the North. Sentries left at night. The CO reported to Roy. Comm. at Roy Divn[?]. Headr. Lingoff with a view to taking over this part. 20 men arrived from transport.	
			Staff: 1 Officer of Essex rejoined. 2 officers of Essex have been kny from [?]. The day was fine and warm	
	Thursday 11 May		Capt. W. O. CAMPBELL and 2/Lieut. J. JACKSON & 2/Lt. ____ at 7:30 pm. by the Ros Grenadiers. 1 N.C.O. killed & 3 wounded by the 2nd Essex in Battalion were relieved by _____ of Essex at 10:10 pm & marched proceeded to _____ .The day was fine & warm	A9

ANNE DUBIN SOUTH

WAR DIARY or INTELLIGENCE SUMMARY

Army Form C. 2118.

Place	Date	Hour	Summary of Events and Information	Remarks and references to Appendices
	1916 Friday 5th May		The Battalion supplies the usual working parties from ANNEQUIN SOUTH and also to two additional recc. Capt. T.H. CAMPBELL and 2/Lieut J.A. JACKSON were buried in CAMBRIN Churchyard at 7.30 pm. also two others with them. The enemy got very little rest or sleep. The day was very close & sultry. JG
	Saturday 6th May		The Battalion supplies the usual working parties and also as of officers & 50 to recc. at BEUVRY. The enemy shelled the 7/KOYLI Battery position at the east end of the village with 5.9" shells. Relief of O.C. Coys. was held & to R.O. decided to cease firing to the rifle gren. of to Brigadier the seniors state of affairs which Everton it to Battalion and of task of NCOs and men.

WAR DIARY or INTELLIGENCE SUMMARY

Army Form C. 2118.

Place	Date	Hour	Summary of Events and Information	Remarks and references to Appendices
	Saturday 8th May 1916		Accordingly framed a memorandum to that effect, here with & sent away this morning. This regimen has recently been from stores. The day was quiet & uneventful.	
	Sunday 7th May		The Second in Command, and the Adjutant and to-day visited the Brie in Vachy Right with a view to taking over tomorrow. The CO had an interview with the Brigadier on the subject of the reasons of the Battalion and the lack of NCOs. The Brigadier said that all that could be done was to bring its matter to the notice of higher authorities.	
	Monday 8th May		A Programme for work during the day was submitted. Capt J. WATT is out of go to this leave and went into hospital the Battalion relieving the 3rd Worcesters in Vachy Right at 10.15 pm. The day was cold and unsettled	Sgg

WAR DIARY or INTELLIGENCE SUMMARY

Army Form C. 2118.

Place	Date	Hour	Summary of Events and Information	Remarks and references to Appendices
	Tuesday 9th May 1916		A very quiet day to the whole. The enemy showed little activity with rifle grenades or artillery and we sustained no casualties. We organised to rifle grenade batteries in our line so as to get best effect. The batteries were under the control of my commander to ensure altered to be "stand to" and were alerted to day was wet & foggy.	
	Wednesday 10th May		The day was quiet on the whole. The war was killed by a rifle grenade on the right bay. A new situations arrived from Scotland and were posted to each company. An organised bombardment was announced of that whole objective the Egypt subsector commencing at 4.30 pm with 4 allow to enemy believe that we intended to make the day was bright sunny [NG]	

Place	Date	Hour	Summary of Events and Information	Remarks and references to Appendices
Thursday	19/10		In consequence of a change in the Division, the Battalion will not be relieved until 14th instant. It is intended that each Brigade should be in the tion for 24 days and for 12. This means that the men will be in the tion clothes for 24 days without and opportunity of getting baths or clean days again of the regimental officers is not asked. the day was quiet in the afternoon. I to Yptanor explored a mine to the enemy was followed by an intense bombardment on our right. This was followed on both sides in which it appeared the heat to the right hand. Work was continued on the trenches, making over head cover as protection against rifle grenades and during all along the front. The day was warm & fine.	JG

WAR DIARY
or
INTELLIGENCE SUMMARY

Army Form C. 2118.

Place	Date	Hour	Summary of Events and Information	Remarks and references to Appendices
	Friday 18th May		Lieut R.G.M. LOUDON was killed this morning about 3am. He had been out in front wiring and had stayed rather long, just as dawn was breaking a sniper got him. The Germans kept very quiet in our front, practically no rifle grenades were used against us. A new revolver gun was used against our bombers today to enemy. The artillery fired at it and got 5 direct hits on it. It is hoped this destroyed it. In intermittent took place to HOHEN ZOLLERN Front Trench. met SC9	
	Saturday 13th May		The day was quiet on the whole. The rain was very slight had rain all the day and night. the 2nd Worcesters went up & Coy Commanders of to trenches with a view of taking over the following day. The day was dull and unsettled SC9	

Army Form C. 2118.

WAR DIARY
or
INTELLIGENCE SUMMARY.
(Erase heading not required.)

Place	Date	Hour	Summary of Events and Information	Remarks and references to Appendices
	Sunday 16th May		The morning was fairly quiet, but in the afternoon our artillery opened on the HOHENZOLLERN front to the part into which the enemy had effected an entrance this was the signal for an intense bombardment by both sides which caused several lives to get to pieces of it, which did not much was annoying. The enemy shelled ANNEQUIN North and South and also to FOSSE. They shelled to 18 par batteries behind CAMBRIN with lachrymatory shells. They exploded a mine just north of the BASEL Rd. which did no damage. We were relieved by 2nd Worcesters in "ACHY" 2gds at 10.30 p.m. and proceeded to billets in both Reserve in ANNEQUIN SOUTH. The day was beautiful and cha..	229

WAR DIARY or INTELLIGENCE SUMMARY

Army Form C. 2118.

Place	Date	Hour	Summary of Events and Information	Remarks and references to Appendices
	Tuesday 15th May		We supplied the usual working parties from ANNEQUIN SOUTH. The day was very quiet, and there was spent in cleaning up billets which had been left in a pretty condition, and in making all of the footpaths in the _____ village. The Quartermaster went to Gorre to Festhard _____ weather fair.	
	Tuesday 16th May		Battalion was relieved by W. Bn. CAMERONIANS at 9 p.m. in turn & battalion proceeded to billets in ANNEZIN. Weather warm & fine.	
	Wednesday 17th		Cleaning up of billets and equipment. Very warm day.	
	Thursday 18th		Parades as per scheme of training.	
	Friday 19th		Parades as normal. Very warm. Three Platoon tournament in evening. Four best men picked to represent 100 M.G.C.	
	Saturday 20.		Parades as yesterday. Very warm. Lieut. GRAY went on leave to Scotland. 2/Lt CHRISTIE acting adjutant during his absence.	

Place	Date	Hour	Summary of Events and Information	Remarks and references to Appendices
	Sunday 21 May		Church Parade for all Corps + Officers in Cinema Hall at 10.30. Very warm + clear	
	Monday 22 May		Parades all day. Battalion began Competition in evening. 9 men selected to shoot against the 100th Inf. Bgde M.G.C. in Bgde contest	
	Tuesday 23 May		Route March. Sgt ANNEZIN 5.45 AM returning about 10.30 AM. Five men fell out on march. Warm & clear. Played M.G.C. two stone men in three bouts of the Sgt were disqualified. Major A.G. Graham goes on leave to Scotland	
	Wednesday 24		Company rifle transfers	
	Thursday 25		Warm for A+B Corps. Gone very chill in C+D Brigade began Competition at 4 am. Battalion won three events at 5 bit and me second prize. Showers all day. 2Lt K.S. Miller goes on leave	
	Friday 26		Parades a morning. Staff holiday for Battalion except in evening. Battalion Orders for malformation. With 5th Suthol Rifle arrived	

Place	Date	Hour	Summary of Events and Information	Remarks and references to Appendices
Sept. 27th			At 11.30 C.O had an interview with Brig. Gen Robertson O/C 19th Brigade Lt. Col. Douglas O/C 5th. Battalion. Actual numbers required by latter not definitely known, will be notified later. No main attack the day in known. Movement orders generally the same. In main relied instructions to moved to Frandean in the afternoon to Le Quesnoy and by night. All previous orders had been cancelled. Recd received instructions to proceed to Sensrahan on Monday 29th. Willette party tomorrow morning. 1st of Nov. 5th S.R. inmigrated that number of men required will be sixty six and twelve officers fifteen chosen during the last few days to distilleries of them. C/SM one will give one the present strength. Lt. J. Denholm goes on leave to Scotland. Entries note made in name and Battalion parts finished in the afternoon.	
Sunday 28			Church Parade at 11 A.M. Mr C.O. went over to HQrs 100th Bt Bale in afternoon + arranged that the twelve officers attached to the 5th S.R. shall remain with us until further notice. Major Boyd went to Pushettes by billette improve in morning. 9 H.L.I. billett party	

WAR DIARY
INTELLIGENCE SUMMARY

Army Form C. 2118.

Place	Date	Hour	Summary of Events and Information	Remarks and references to Appendices
	Sunday 26		Arrived here in numerous temporary billets. Have a thousand men the whole of the 100th Bde is still out of the transport are active as a reserve to the 15th Division pro-tem. As the enemy are reported the measures for the 15th Division front — CAPT RAWLINS RAMC returned from leave. Bright hot day.	
	Monday 29		Bn paraded at 8.30 a.m. were marched to BEAUVRY Bn will be attached to the 5th S.R. at 12.15. Battalion marched. Whole of them into temporary billets at small village of BUSHETTES. A, B, C & D Coys into temporary billets in BUSHETTES. Remainder of Battalion into temporary billets near by LE HAMEL. Remainder of 2/7th Royal Warwicks & new battalion pending removal of 2/7th Royal Warwicks a new battalion put out. Very hot day.	
	Tuesday 30		Royal Warwicks moved out to LEPREOL at 12.15 and A, B, C & D Coys took over their billets. Orders received to send 121 men to 15th Bn THE CAMERONIANS and 198 men to 18th Bn Middlesex Regt. Watch rain last night and dense down afternoon. heat of Company Commanders at 11.30 A.M. to discuss numbers to be left him each Company at 10.30 p.m. orders arrived to attach 150 more men to the 251st Tunnelling Company in lieu of

Place	Date	Hour	Summary of Events and Information	Remarks and references to Appendices
	Wednesday 31st		At 9 A.M. 121 men were sent to the 1st Bn. CAMERONIANS and 296 men to the 1st Bn. MIDDLESEX REGT. All the men were addressed by the C.O. before leaving. At 10.30 the C.O. rode to BETHUNE to see G.O.C. 33rd Division regarding the inability to send the 150 men called for tomorrow, the matter is now under consideration. At 3 p.m. Cast night's orders re the 150 men was cancelled. Capt GRAY returned from leave. Warm and cloudy day.	

www.ingramcontent.com/pod-product-compliance
Lightning Source LLC
Chambersburg PA
CBHW080838010526
44114CB00017B/2332